GET YOUR PLAY ON

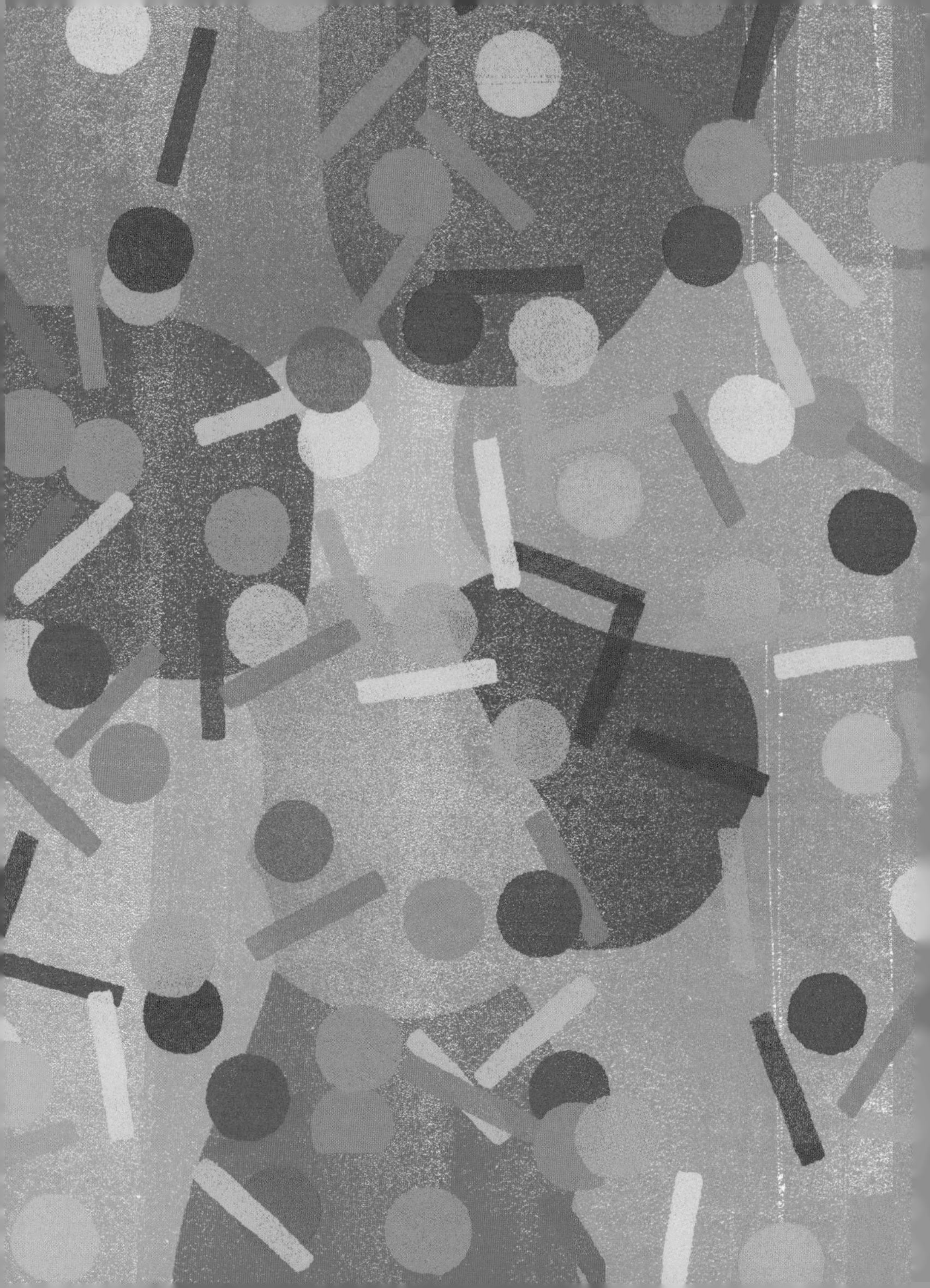

CORALIE SLEAP
WITH LAURA BAYLISS

GET YOUR PLAY ON

CREATIVE WAYS TO HAVE FUN IN A SERIOUS WORLD

HarperCollins*Publishers*

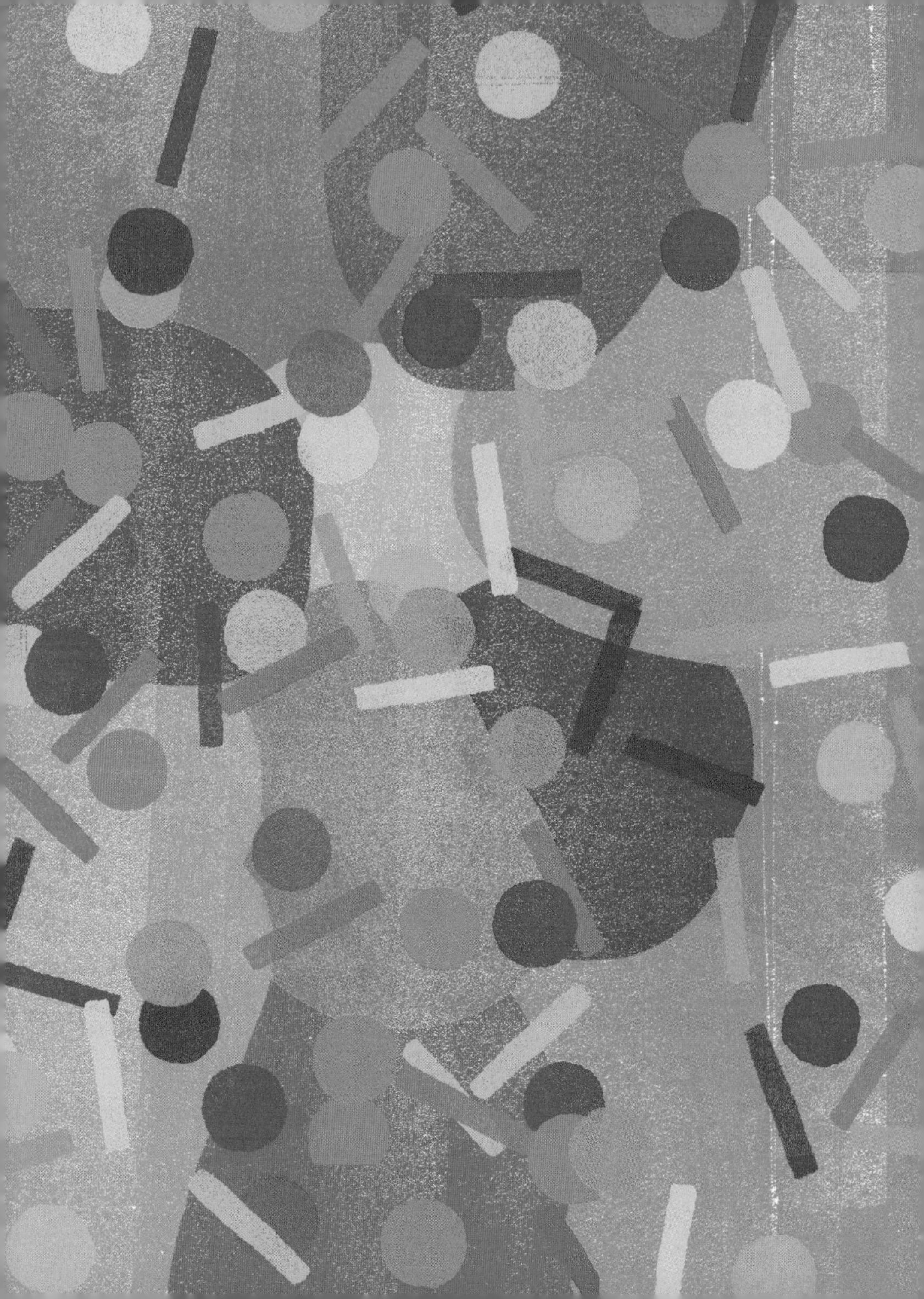

CONTENTS

Art Club!

After leaving uni, and in a quest to bring more playfulness back into their lives, Coralie Sleap and her housemates started a midweek house party for their bored and broke friends. They called it Art Club. It provided welcome respite from their office jobs and took them back to the spontaneous, creative highs of their art school days. Art Club changed topics. Sometimes they really spent time learning a new skill; sometimes they just did a few creative warm-up exercises; but always they just had a bash at stuff with no pressure to make any kind of salvageable outcome. Sometimes, they forgot to make anything and just had a massive party with crayons in cocktails.

Friends soon asked if they could bring their colleagues – 'outsiders' – to Art Club. If the original group had been missing being creative for a few months, these lawyers and academics lit up at their first opportunity to be creative without pressure since primary school. Coralie knew creativity made her happy, but seeing how easy it was to bring this joy to many others was even more rewarding. She had found her calling.

Sitting at a laptop all day and living for the weekend was beginning to nag at her soul, and when her dad was taken critically ill, it gave her a sudden perspective on how important it was to be spending your time doing something meaningful. Something that brought you joy.

So, after leaving her job and spending some quality time at home, it became apparent that 2008 was not a great year for landing dream jobs. The doom and gloom of a city in the midst of a post-financial crisis made the desire for a haven of inspirational happiness even more attractive. And just at that point an opportunity with a visionary landlord, an empty property and an old school friend led to a pop-up creativity and cocktail club being conceived. And people loved it!

In 2009, Drink, Shop & Do opened its doors in a beautiful bathhouse in King's Cross. Three floors of weird and wonderful things to make, learn and DO were all helped along by banging cocktails, cakes and DJs. Drink, Shop & Do has hosted over 5,000 events; won Design My Night best venue in King's Cross year after year; have been selected as *Time Out*'s top five clubs; been featured in newspapers and magazines from New York to Japan; hosted celebrity parties and DJs; and has been shortlisted for a Bar & Restaurant Design award, among many other accolades for its innovative approach.

Life is far too short to be bored. It's time we start taking play seriously.

For a decade, it has been the venue for countless counterculture craft events, inventive first dates, and a place for stressed-out urbanites to come, unwind and remember that life is to be enjoyed. From Freddie Mercury clay parties (where everyone sculpts their own mini icon to take home) to the highly competitive LEGO Robots competition and not-to-be-dunked-at Lionel Rich-Tea biscuit decorating night, this is no ordinary knitting circle. Strangers have become friends, romances have blossomed and there are even some regular LEGO aficionados who have met each month.

To help you forget the rat race and embrace being the fun-loving genius you are, Drink, Shop & Do is sharing its ultimate book of play.

Each chapter in this colourful, creative emporium of an interactive, inspirational megatome, focuses on one key aspect of play; the five main playtime 'skills' that are the unintended beneficial consequences of having more fun: Create, Connect, Imagine, Think and Move.

Through more than 100 tips and activities, discover how thinking more playfully can improve your relationships and how you can unlock your dream future, connect with those around you, be more playful as you go about your day-to-day chores and see your neighbourhood from a fresh perspective. There are also contributions from worldwide Experts in Play – from an artist and theatre company to a parkour expert – each explaining how you can reap the benefits by celebrating your more playful side.

How many times have you felt more nourished and recharged after time spent being silly with your friends, than after another evening lounging on the sofa, an intense spin class or even an expensive spa treatment? Sometimes all we need to turn our week around is to don our (possibly wonky) creative hat and have a good laugh.

Life is pretty serious right now. It's hard to listen to the news without feeling deflated and alone in our worries. But worrying is not good for our health; it makes us less productive and retreating into isolation makes us feel increasingly disconnected. We're spending too much time on our phones and staring at screens and our health and sleep are suffering. (Although, technology is not all bad and we will explore ways in which it can benefit our lives and help us feel more playful . . .) Playful people have more fun. Play can help us to forget our worries for a while, and adopting a more playful attitude means we're better able to cope with life's ups and downs. Self-care is a big buzzword right now, but sometimes it's all rather introspective, prioritising pampering baths and manicures over more enriching activities. There's time for baths and colourful nails, but sometimes it's hard to switch off our whirring minds when we're alone in our thoughts.

But let's not overcomplicate things or make it too serious. Let's just try to bring a bit more positivity and playfulness into our approach to life. Watch how that positivity spreads – fun is infectious.

We are all fun, creative people, but sometimes in the midst of office politics and life admin, it can get lost along the way. Your day will be far better if you wake up on the fun side of the bed, so let that creative, imaginative, joyful side of you out as you go about your day.

Introduction

Why play?

As children, play comes easily. We think nothing of kicking a ball around, making up complex imaginary worlds with our friends or getting lost in our own thoughts, devoting whole afternoons to sticking, gluing and covering everything with glitter. As adults, though, playtime tends to take a bit of a back seat, or it can be yet another 'thing' in our diaries, a scheduled commitment we feel obliged to fulfil, or another goal to achieve . . .

Playfulness often gets drummed out of us. At school we are told to 'stop messing around and focus'. But play is actually a powerful developmental asset for the brain. It is a trait seen in all cultures worldwide, so it must serve an important evolutionary purpose.

Playtime can be just as beneficial for adults, beyond the pleasure it brings us. It can teach us new skills, allow us to think more creatively and imaginatively, help us problem-solve and strengthen social interactions. Active play – from playing games to making something, to working as a team in a pub quiz – builds relationships, improves lateral thinking and boosts self-esteem.

People who regularly play tend to demonstrate lower stress levels and a better ability to cope with life's demands – it literally makes us more fun to be around. And animal studies show that those who play could have a better chance of survival and may be more attractive to a mate – so play could be viewed as a life and death situation!

The best thing about play is that it expects nothing from you, but its effects can be long-lasting and far-reaching. Play doesn't care if your self-portrait looks more like Ryan Gosling, or your LEGO spaceship has a dinosaur riding on its back and no windows. And it will cheer you on excitedly as you miss every shot at goal. And who says what's good anyway? There's no judgement here. It's purely for fun, remember . . .

When you're in the moment, doing something you're really enjoying, you get into that much-revered state of flow psychologists suggest we should try to find ourselves in as often as possible. You've turned off any self-consciousness. You've dropped your guard, your ego, stopped overthinking everything. Play allows our minds to switch off from our day-to-day worries so we can connect more deeply with ourselves, which can result in some surprising insights.

Play is not for Instagram; it's purely for fun and joy in the moment. You don't even have to be any good at it!

There are countless ways to bring more playfulness into your everyday – and endless ways to reap the benefits too. Perhaps the most familiar way we understand playtime is through physical games. As adults, we all know about the good things exercise can bring us – better physical health, a rush of endorphins and, if we're with other people, a lovely bonding feeling. But movement is about more than just getting blood circulating, it can help us see our environment differently, appreciate nature and our surroundings, and boost our confidence.

In fact, giving ourselves a much-needed fist pump is one of the unifying benefits of all types of play. When we set aside time to do something purely for the fun of it, when we finish, we feel that warm glow of achievement. Time well spent.

We shouldn't set out to play simply in order to achieve; that's not the point at all. But we should know that playtime most definitely isn't wasted time. The more playful we are, the more fun we are. And the more fun we are, suddenly the more enjoyable life becomes.

Let it flow

Before we get into the ways in which different types of play can enhance your life, there's one benefit that all play can provide: flow.

What is FLOW?

Being in a state of flow is all about 'getting into the zone'. It's that magical state when you feel like you are effortlessly moving from one moment to the next, being fully involved in the task at hand. Everything is going exactly as you had hoped. Creativity has landed. The muse is here! You know that feeling when you're so caught up in what you're doing that you don't notice time passing, you don't remember to eat lunch, your breathing is calm and steady, and you're not worrying about any of life's day-to-day inevitable annoyances? That's flow. Being in a state of flow shuts down our (often noisy) inner critic as we focus only on the now, and in doing so we are able to connect more deeply with ourselves. It is like a form of active meditation (see page 200) and the amazing thing is, we can get into this state with very little effort. And, also like meditation, regularly achieving a state of flow has

= joy

been linked to greatly improved general wellbeing and happiness.

Basically, flow helps you to unlock your inner creativity and imagination; it's where energy and thoughts flow uninterrupted; it's where you're aware of what you're doing but are fully concentrating only on being right in the moment. You lose a sense of your ego, your self-consciousness, and for a while you're just in a blissful state of 'doing', where the process of your activity can become more enjoyable and more important than the end result. You can develop and build skills in flow, which can in turn improve your self-confidence. It results in increased productivity and deeper thinking, as you indulge in one focused task at a time – instead of the multi-tasking nightmare of our daily to-do lists. Those who regularly reach a state of flow have also been shown to be much more productive in other areas of their work and home life, too, as they become better at concentrated focus.

'A good life is one that is characterised by complete absorption in what one does.' Mihaly Csikszentmihalyi

As children, we probably reached a state of flow most days – getting lost in our made-up worlds as we drew fantasy lands over reams of paper or built elaborate playgrounds for our pet hamster out of empty cereal boxes and toilet roll tubes. As adults, though, we tend to

HIGH

AROUSAL
(Alert, Focused)

ANXIETY
(Stressed, Alert)

FLOW
(Focused, Happy)

CHALLENGES

WORRY
(Stressed, Alert)

CONTROL
(Happy, Confident)

BOREDOM
(Depressed, Contented)

RELAXATION
(Confident, Contented)

APATHY
(Sad, Depressed)

LOW ← ABILITIES → HIGH

become a bit more concerned about 'the point' of doing these kinds of activities – we think we don't have time to spend on creative tasks, unless they serve a greater 'purpose' in our lives or we worry about whether what we produce at the end will be any 'good'.

Getting into a state of flow doesn't have to be through traditionally creative activities, though – playing sports, gardening or even cleaning the bathroom can do the job just as well – but it is thought that making something, or engaging in some kind of physical movement, which also requires you to be completely mentally absorbed, is the quickest way for us to reach a state of flow. When choosing your flow activity, there are a few ideal conditions that will help you reach bliss:

- It has to be an activity you enjoy . . . (OK, kind of obvious.)
- You have to become totally immersed in your activity, which means you have to know what you're doing and what you're going to be doing next. It needs to be at an optimum level of difficulty: not too tricky – you don't want to have to stop to research how to do the next stage – but equally, not so easy that your mind starts wandering off task.
- It should include some challenges, so you see yourself moving on, conquering ground and progressing. And no, making it through to watch the next episode on Netflix does not count here (although progressing to the next level of a computer game can . . .).
- No interruptions or distractions – you need some quality time to get fully in the zone (around half an hour at least) so you can focus only on the task at hand. Phones down.
- The focus is on the process of 'doing' not the end result.

Flow state takes you outside of yourself for a while and allows your inner self to rule. It helps you appreciate being in the now – and aren't we all trying to be a little more mindful these days? Ideally as much of our working life as possible should be in flow state, if we are truly engaged and inspired by what we do . . . It's a sure way to reduce stress and anxiety and provide a fast track to happiness as you let go of your day-to-day drama, at least for a little bit.

Five fast tracks to flow

Make something

We often hear stories of artists and writers being so caught up in their creative endeavour, they work through frenzied days and nights for a week to finish a project. Find something you really enjoy doing and let it take you out of yourself for a while – painting, drawing, sewing, papier-mâchéing models of your dog, building a LEGO fort, writing dirty limericks – whatever it is, make it yours. You'll find lots of ideas for 'hands-on projects' throughout this book to help you find your state of flow.

Music

If you are lucky enough to play a musical instrument, music is one of the best ways to reach a state of flow. So, dig out that old recorder and get going on 'Greensleeves'! Or compose your next masterpiece and play it to your plants.

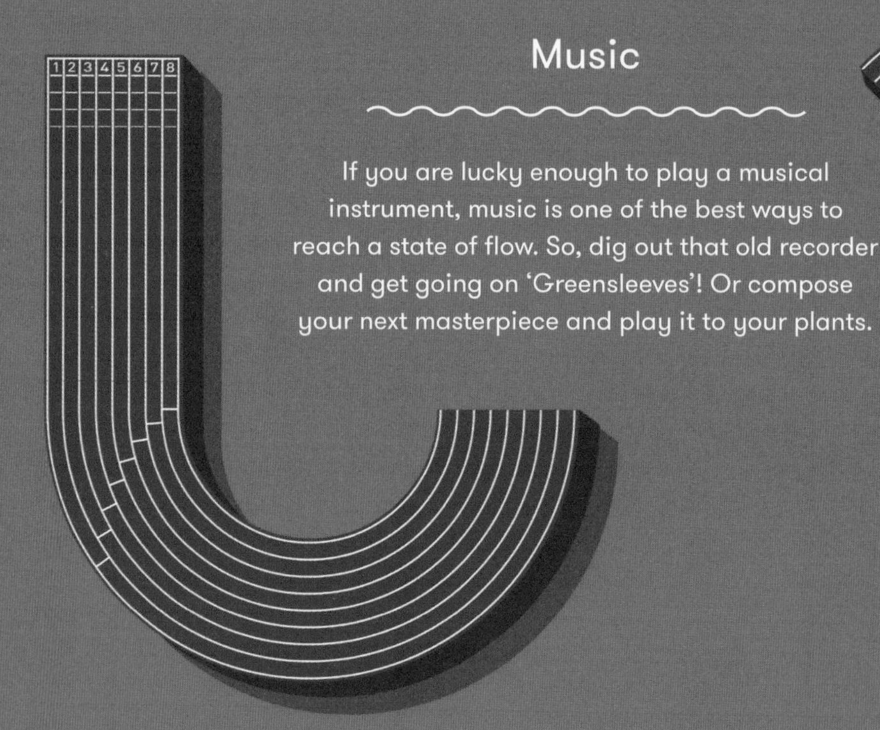

Puzzling

Crosswords, sudoku, jigsaws, anagrams, dot-to-dots – as long as they get you immersed and fully engaged, puzzles of all kinds can get you flowing along in no time. (See page 196 more on the benefits of puzzling, plus some starter ideas, from our Expert in Play.)

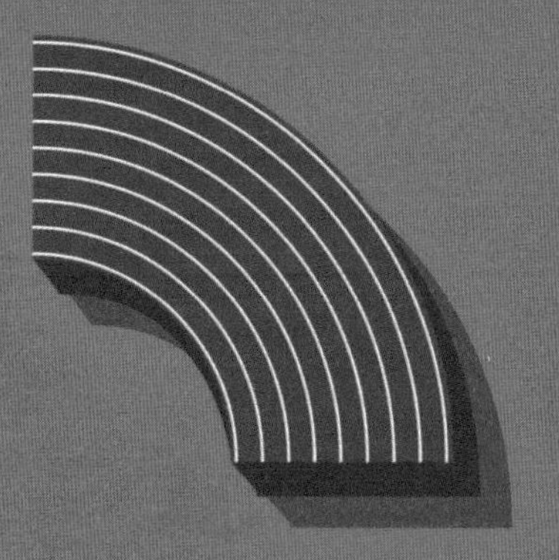

Video games

Because of their 'levelling up' design, based around clear goals and instant feedback (you either jump that bridge or you don't), video games are actually really good ways to quickly get into a state of flow. In fact, game designers Jenova Chen and Nicholas Clark even developed a game called 'Flow' based on research into flow states.

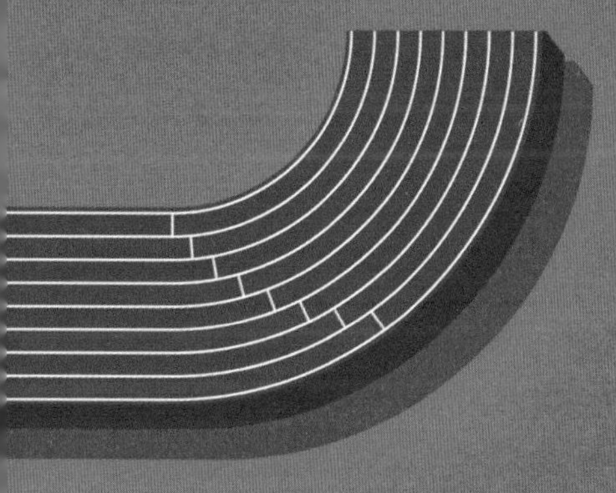

Physical activities

These tend to use a range of skills, from mentally working out your next move to using your body in new, challenging ways, and they can very effectively get you into a flow state. Try mountain biking, rock climbing, dancing and team sports.

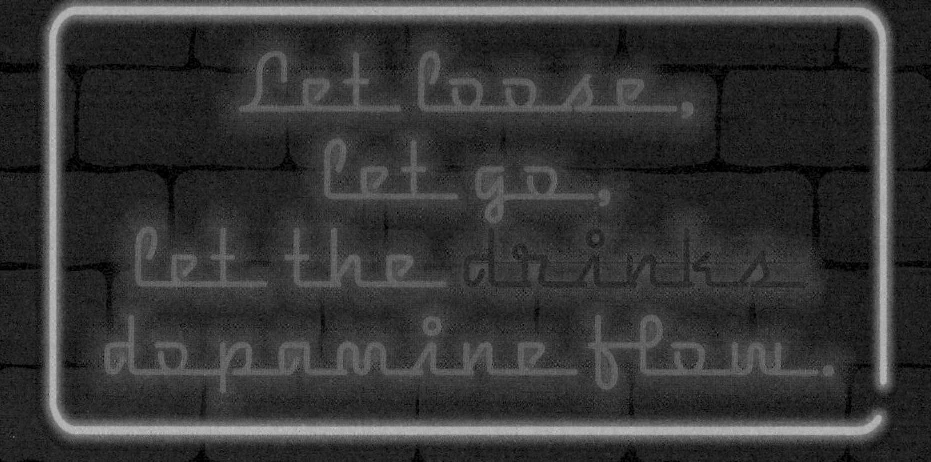

The hormone dopamine operates along the reward pathways in our brain, encouraging us to seek new experiences. It lets us anticipate how an outcome will make us feel, which drives us towards or away from that activity as part of our survival instincts.

It's what gives us that 'YES! Fist-pump-the-air' feeling when we achieve something or do something that makes us feel good. Too little dopamine has been linked to feeling unmotivated and depressed, whereas too much dopamine has been associated with schizophrenia and making connections between things that don't exist. So our body tends to keep us in a good, even balance.

There are plenty of well-documented ways to get a quick fix of dopamine. You could go binge-drinking! Hit the casino then take home the nearest willing stranger. (NB, these are not advised.) All will get dopamine rushing through your veins. But alas, with these highs come terrible, terrible lows. That low that hangs over you for days when it all seems pointless? That's a right bummed-out level of dopamine. We all know that to live a happy, playful life we need a steady balance, so try these for a natural, steady dopamine lift.

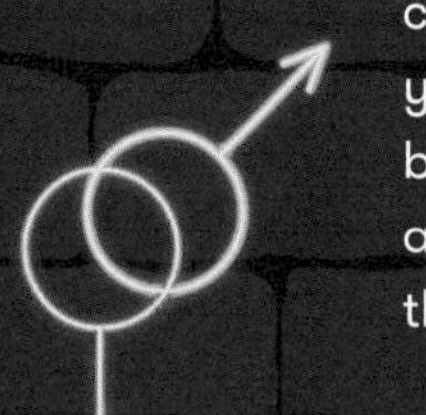

Eat protein

Proteins contain amino acids, in particular tyrosine and phenylalanine, which have been linked to dopamine production. So eat lots of protein-rich foods like lean meats, fish, dairy, nuts, seeds, tofu and pulses.

Other dopamine-boosting foods

Eat bananas, nuts, dark chocolate, oily fish, green tea and watermelon.

Physical touch

Hug someone, stroke your pet or get a massage. Even a nice interaction with someone can give us a lift (see page 72).

Get up early

Studies show that dopamine is produced in large amounts first thing in the morning, so have an early night for creativity at dawn.

Music

Listening to music has been shown to help boost dopamine levels as it quickly activates the reward areas of the brain.

Sunlight

Get outside. Sunlight boosts mood and dopamine. Combine with exercise for a double-whammy power-up. Try new activities – anticipating these can increase dopamine production.

Get creative

Being creative can help get dopamine flowing, so start with some simple creative exercises (see pages 38, 42 and 54).

Meditation or yoga

The focused attention in meditation works as a repetitive reward cycle. You can see benefits from a few minutes a week (see page 200).

1

CREATE

I remember when I was a little girl, all I wanted to do was make things. Colourful paintings. Cut out collages. Lots of things with egg boxes and glue. It sticks clearly in my mind the day a friend's mum put a limit on how much paper I could use.

I had a sudden awareness that she coveted the colourful paper for the resource it was, not as a means to an end for making something. We hadn't run out of it, like we did in my house, it was considered too precious to use. I froze; at six, I experienced 'blank page' fear. Once learned, it took years to unlearn. I suddenly felt the precious value of the resource I was using. What if what I made wasn't any good? What if I ruined that precious paper? Blank page fear is the enemy of the carefreeness needed to be playful and creative.

Being creative can get lost early on. When I look back at times when I haven't been making things, they've been quite unhappy moments. Everyone needs an outlet, otherwise something inside us gets trapped, spinning around our conscious brain and making us crazy. You might have forgotten how your creativity shows itself, but as a child you would have leaned into something. As humans we have always sought to make our mark, ever since we figured out we could scratch a rock against a cave wall; something by which others could acknowledge the existence of our soul. Whether it was writing, colouring, music or dance, something would have called to you. Think back to those early days of making things, before you compared your output with others. When you were proud to gift your scribbles to your loved ones' fridge.

The enemy of creativity is stress, but it turns out that the kryptonite of stress is creativity. When our brains are full of to-do lists and pressures, deadlines and worries, creativity is usually the first thing to go. We need to feel safe and secure to let the deep imaginings of our soul emerge into the world. When we're out of practice it's scary – we can be so judgy that, even if we know no one else will see or hear us, we still don't let it pour out easily. I find being alone is often the best way to put me in the creative zone. When my busy life feels a little joyless, I'll look back and realise it is because every minute of my colour-coded time-blocked diary (see page 195) is full – even if it includes fun things, like dinner with friends. There is no time for rest. And it's in the rested body and mind, almost at the point of boredom, that your mind clicks into what you'd like to do. Jump on this feeling: grab this moment. It can be tempting to use this energy for socialising, or mindlessly browsing YouTube. That might be enough to placate the mind but it certainly doesn't feed the soul. Instead, take down some barriers and re-engage with your creativity.

What was it you used to like doing? Dig that guitar out of your parents' loft, or buy yourself some new oil pastels. Leave them in a place where you relax. Plan in some rest time to do exactly what you feel in that moment. It might not be a still life – this week it might be to dance weirdly in the kitchen. Fill a sketchbook: turn the pages quickly and don't look back and judge. This isn't about being perfect – in fact, it's quite the opposite. This is all just a warm-up. Don't get caught up in making something you are proud of. Just be proud you did it.

Although this outpouring may not seem a valuable use of your precious time, what it is doing is building new pathways in your brain. And physically, you are becoming more dexterous, which is a use-it-or-lose-it skill. We all want to be more agile in later life, but instead we spend our days hunched over laptops. And in having to make unobvious choices, in having to muster something out of the nothingness, we dig into our subconscious, bringing out things we didn't know we had within ourselves. When you have no expectations, the results are always a pleasant surprise. So, when you build seemingly 'pointless' activities into your packed schedule, you are allowing your brain to develop. Then when you're faced with problems in the real world, you'll join the dots that someone else won't even see.

So, get a proper night's sleep and get hydrated. Put your tools in front of you. Stay still and take some deep breaths. Look inward without forcing it. If you've put pressure on yourself and nothing is coming, do some of the quick-fire activities overleaf and get things flowing. But most of all, enjoy creating something purely for the process of creating it. For once, it's really not about the end result.

Do you doodle?

Doodling is an easy, no-pressure way to instantly get those creative juices flowing. Bill Gates doodles, Thomas Edison doodled, American presidents doodle – we all should be doing more doodling! There are loads of benefits to be gained from doodling.

It's a great way to destress, it can help you solve a nagging problem and it can also boost your concentration. A 2009 study from Plymouth University found that shading in shapes helped people retain 29 per cent more information when listening to a boring phone conversation. The idea behind this is that doodling keeps your brain from wandering too far away from the task at hand by giving it something else to focus on and stop you actually disappearing into a daydream. (Not that daydreaming should be discouraged – see page 162 for how to enhance your daydreaming skills.)

Scribbling across your notes at work is not wasted time. It's a brilliant way to activate your creativity and encourage abstract thinking – it can help you to see the broader picture and think more expansively. By doing something with your hands and creating something visual, you're also stimulating the visual part of your brain, which can help you 'see' your problems from a different perspective and give you fresh insight when you are mulling something over. In fact, a brief wander down Doodle Street could be just what you need to help kick-start thinking more creatively so you can solve that big dilemma.

Exactly *what* you doodle can also reveal a lot about you – from your motivations to your most secret desires.

The most common doodles tend to involve abstract patterns, random shapes, objects, animals and letters. According to Tracey Trussell, a professional doodle and handwriting analyst, flowers can mean you're loyal, stars show ambition (but also impatience), zigzags that you have a daring personality and triangles that you will stop at nothing in the quest for your goals.

Criss-cross lines can indicate an anxious nature, circles show kindness, while wavy lines suggest an adaptable, quick thinker who can also be indecisive.

Large doodles are for those who like to be in the limelight, while smaller doodles are for the more modest among us. If you regularly

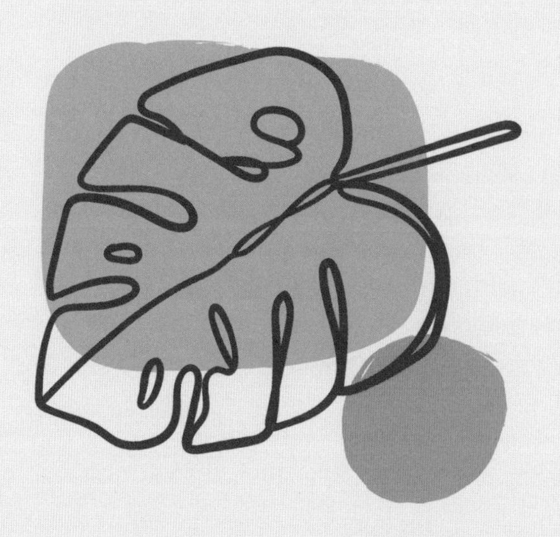

draw faces, well, unsurprisingly this shows you're a people person.

And while doodling in the same spot can be a sign of anxiety . . . it can also be a sign of guilt. If you draw cubes or 3D objects, you are clearly a clever bean and enjoy seeing the bigger picture and other people's perspectives.

So, next time you find your pen meandering across the top of your to-do list, remember you're in good company and could be about to come up with your most creative idea yet.

Child psychologist D.W. Winnicott used 'the squiggle game' to learn more about his clients. They would take it in turns to draw a random squiggle, then the other person would carry on the drawing, elaborating on it to produce whatever they felt like. They would then tell stories to each other about their drawings, which would reveal to Winnicott insights into what his client was thinking.

Just get your pen moving. What do you see in this ink blob? Can you make it into something? And don't be afraid to turn the page upside down to see things from another perspective.

Fill up this room with
a dreamy vase of flowers,
a crazy pattern wallpaper, a
shaggy rug and maybe
a sunset view ...

Embracing imperfection

When things get a bit uncomfortable, we can have our best ideas. One of the easiest ways to kill creativity before it's got started is to give in to our obsession with perfection. Artists will almost always begin with a rough idea scribbled randomly in their sketchbooks, and writers work on countless drafts; no one sees all the half-finished attempts that are crossed out, screwed up and dramatically thrown in the bin.

There's beauty to be appreciated in the imperfect. In recent years we've (thankfully) started to reject mass-produced, samey products in favour of hand-crafted, individual pieces, which all come with their own unique marks: ink that has spontaneously landed or splattered over a design, a rogue bubble that formed in the kiln, uneven stitching on our handmade sofa cushions or the wiggly edge of a beloved bowl. And we all love the dog with the wonky ear . . .

It's only natural that in our day-to-day lives we try to avoid errors as far as we can, constantly trying to balance work, family and personal goals, and to at least give the appearance that everything is under control, thank you very much. We spin all these plates with circus-skill expertise. But by doing this we're ignoring the fact that it's all those imperfections that we try to cover up that make us the amazing, unique individuals we really are. Our less-than-perfect aspects teach us more about ourselves – and actually many of them are much more fun than the neatly managed areas of our lives. Who doesn't love a bit of chaos now and then – it's in the chaos the fun stuff happens, right? Random nights out where you don't know where you'll end up, friendships made in unexpected places, weird dinners from the corner shop eaten in the park on the last sunny day of the year, bright and brilliant ideas that come out of nowhere. This is where real life is hiding – not inside your Marie Kondo'ed sock drawer.

It can be difficult to enjoy what we perceive to be our less-than-ideal qualities, or to set out to do something without worrying about the outcome. But that's what being more playful is all about – having a go and enjoying the process. Creativity is about creating, so get started and see where you end up. People don't become experts overnight – it can take years to hone skills. But there's pleasure to be found in the mistakes, and learning to be enjoyed from making revisions. Once you embrace imperfection, you'll find there's even more beauty in all things uniquely off-centre and life won't seem so serious.

Balls it up and have a ball

Look around you right now and draw across these pages the perfectly imperfect that exists in your world – it could be your favourite unsymmetrical houseplant that has all its flowers blooming on one side, or a messy meal you enjoyed eating that got sauce all down your t-shirt, or you could reacquaint yourself with a handmade gift that you love all the more because that bit on the back doesn't quite join up to the bit on the side like it 'should' . . .

Test your tolerance of imperfection and realise it's really not the end of the world if things go a bit wonky from time to time. Go wild and put a few forks in the spoons section of your cutlery drawer, plate up your dinner in an un-Instagram-worthy fashion, apply a face mask and – gasp – spread it unevenly around your eyes. Draw something carefully and neatly – and then ruin it by scribbling over it or adding a rude speech bubble. Challenge yourself to break with convention, flex those feelings of discomfort – and know that the sky won't come crashing down around you.

It's impossible to draw a perfect circle, so fill the imperfect rounds on this page with drawings to celebrate all things misshapen.

Hands on

With so much of our modern world existing online, many of us are losing the skills of making things with our hands. For some, even our handwriting has taken a horrible turn since primary school, because we don't tend to write more than a shopping list with an actual pen.

But there's an important neurological link between our hands and brain, which is why we often find simple repetitive physical tasks relaxing and satisfying – like doing the ironing, washing-up or untangling a big ball of wool or knotted necklace. Neuroscientist Kelly Lambert has even coined the term 'behaviorceuticals', because she believes that when we do something physical, we can change the neurochemistry of our brains in much the same way that pharmaceuticals can. It's now thought that hands-on activities can encourage increased neuroplasticity, too – so we can actually rewire parts of our brains to think differently as we learn and practise new skills.

Our brains crave creative activities; they meet a basic primal need in all of us – after all, we've been painting things on walls since we lived in caves. And making something comes with the added bonus of having something to show for it at the end. Depending on your skills, it could be something you actually want – like a new knitted hat or portrait of your pet, or a freshly painted bathroom. But don't worry if you haven't quite mastered your chosen technique yet, since that's another benefit of doing things with your hands: you quickly get better at it, which provides another boost to your confidence, wellbeing and happiness.

While our grandmothers took pride in repairing and mending, and Sundays were DIY days for fixing squeaky doors and building treehouses, in our modern throwaway culture – where we send things out to be fixed and order in takeaways, and cheap flat-pack furniture arrives in the post – we all have moments when it feels like life is controlling us, rather than the other way around. Everything is moving very quickly and it can feel like it's getting faster and faster . . . With anxiety and depression on the rise, and an increasing sense of a lack of power over our wider situation when it comes to world events (just watching the news can leave us feeling helpless), Lambert suggests that making things can help us regain a sense of control over our environment and recommends we make time for hands-on activities in our everyday. Simple practical tasks like fixing things, cooking and gardening – even darning socks – can all improve our mental health and make us feel more useful and productive. In the nineteenth

century, doctors even prescribed knitting as an aid for anxious women – at first this seems a ridiculous and outrageously patronising act of the patriarchy, but as Lambert explains, knitting requires us to use several different parts of our brain simultaneously; repetitive tasks are known to activate serotonin pathways; and thinking about the end project is a hopeful, satisfying target. And, when you're absorbed in a creative endeavour – even if it's a more mundane one – it can often be just the moment when great ideas arise as we hit that much-revered flow state (see pages 12–15).

So, when we consider all this, the recent rise in hands-on hobbies, group drawing sessions, baking, making and upcycling are suddenly not that surprising at all. Dissatisfied with our online, abstract worlds, we may be moving towards more physically creative activities to counteract our tap-tap-tapping workadays. Plus, there are the additional benefits of increased physical dexterity as we do close work, and we hone our ability to follow instructions as we see a project through to the end. People who make things are also known to be better at problem-solving, as they work around unexpected difficulties and come up with practical solutions.

Making things with our hands, even something as simple as a batch of flapjacks, has so many benefits to our mental wellbeing. The more you make, the better you feel – you'll be calmer, more in control, and with a sense of achievement, which will leave you more relaxed and receptive to more fun and playfulness.

Hands-on creative flow

As we know, getting handsy is one of the very best ways to reach a state of flow (see page 16). The added benefit of this kind of activity – compared with a more physical one like dancing or rock climbing – is that you end up with something tangible to enjoy when you're done.

Being able to calmly follow instructions is another really useful life skill to master, as is actually sticking with a task and seeing it through to completion. By embarking on a creative hands-on activity you can learn a new skill – or build on existing ones – and feel an amazing sense of achievement.

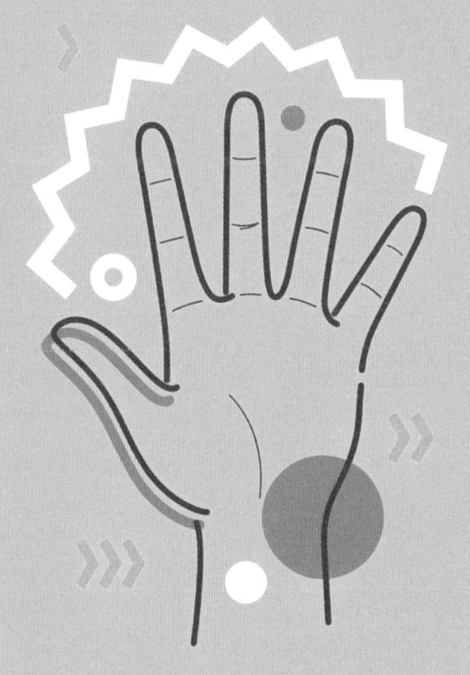

Origami

Master the Japanese art of paper folding, from butterflies to rabbits to dinosaurs. Legend has it that if you fold 1,000 cranes, you will be granted a wish by the Gods. Now, there's an unintended incentive for play if ever we heard one.

Knitting

Gaining popularity as a great stress reliever (see opposite) this is the perfect flow activity. Knit a scarf, hat, gloves or just a pile of misshapen squares and join them up into a new winter blanket.

How to make cactus crafts

Paper cactus craft is loads of fun and a great way to decorate your shelves and windowsills. (Much easier to care for than the real thing!)

You will need

- o Templates (opposite)
- o Scissors
- o Pencil
- o Colourful card or heavy paper (particularly greens)
- o Quick-drying all-purpose glue
- o White or silver gel pen or fine chalk pen

How to make the cactus

1

Cut out the templates.

2

Trace around each template on to coloured card or heavy paper a minimum of three times. Each copy will make one of the 'ridges' of your cactus. The more you have, the more 3D and realistic it looks, but it's also nice to have a variety.

3

Cut them out. You can make up your own shapes too – as long as they are symmetrical.

4

Fold each cactus shape in half lengthways, down the stem.

5

Apply glue to one half of a folded shape, then attach another shape to the first one, almost like you are making a book.

6

Glue on the next shape in the same way (if you are doing more than three, keep going until you have attached them all). When you have attached the final shape, glue the unglued side to the unglued side of the first shape to close up all the sides.

7

Use a white or silver gel pen or chalk pen to make little hairs or spines all over the cactus.

8

Now you've got the hang of it try gluing just rectangle 'pages' together first, then free-hand cut out an asymmetrical cactus with cowboy arms!

How to make the pot

You could always use any cute real pots you have lying around, possibly from failed attempts of keeping real plants alive. Or maybe you've been so successful at keeping real plants that you've had to repot them as they've grown so well. Feel smug about that.

1

Take a piece of A4 card and cut a 3cm strip from the long side. Now cut a 9–10cm circle (you might want to find a mug or small bowl to draw round).

2

Glue the long rectangle around the circle to make a little pot. We found this easier to do with quick-drying glue.

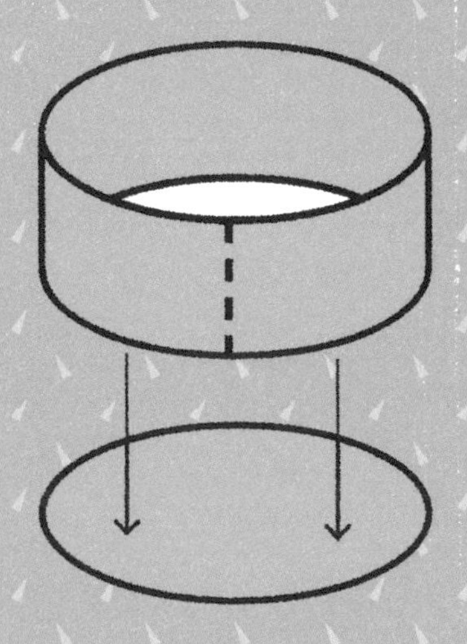

How to pot your cactus

1

Apply glue on the bottom of the cactus, then glue it into your plant pot.

2

Cut out some little cactus flowers to add as a finishing touch.

Macrame plant hanger

Try this brilliant macrame plant hanger by Poppy Schooling.

You will need

- 8 x 3m lengths of cord (you can also use string or wool – work with whatever you've got)
- 1 wooden or brass ring (for hanging)
- 2 x 1.5m lengths of cord

You'll use three knots

Spiral knot

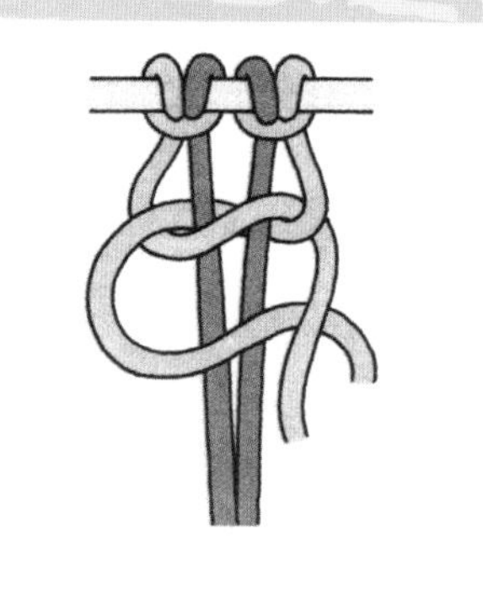

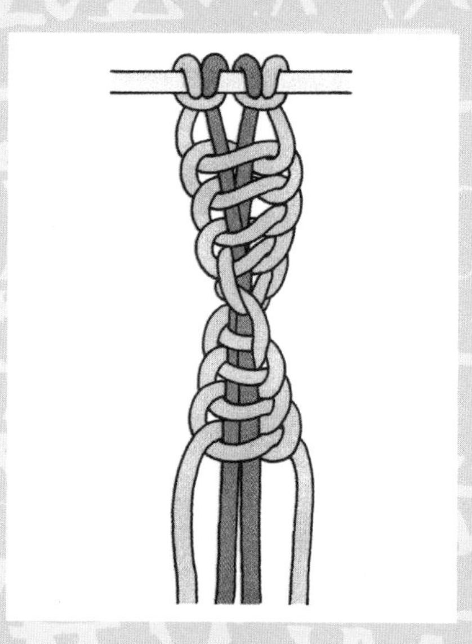

Square knot

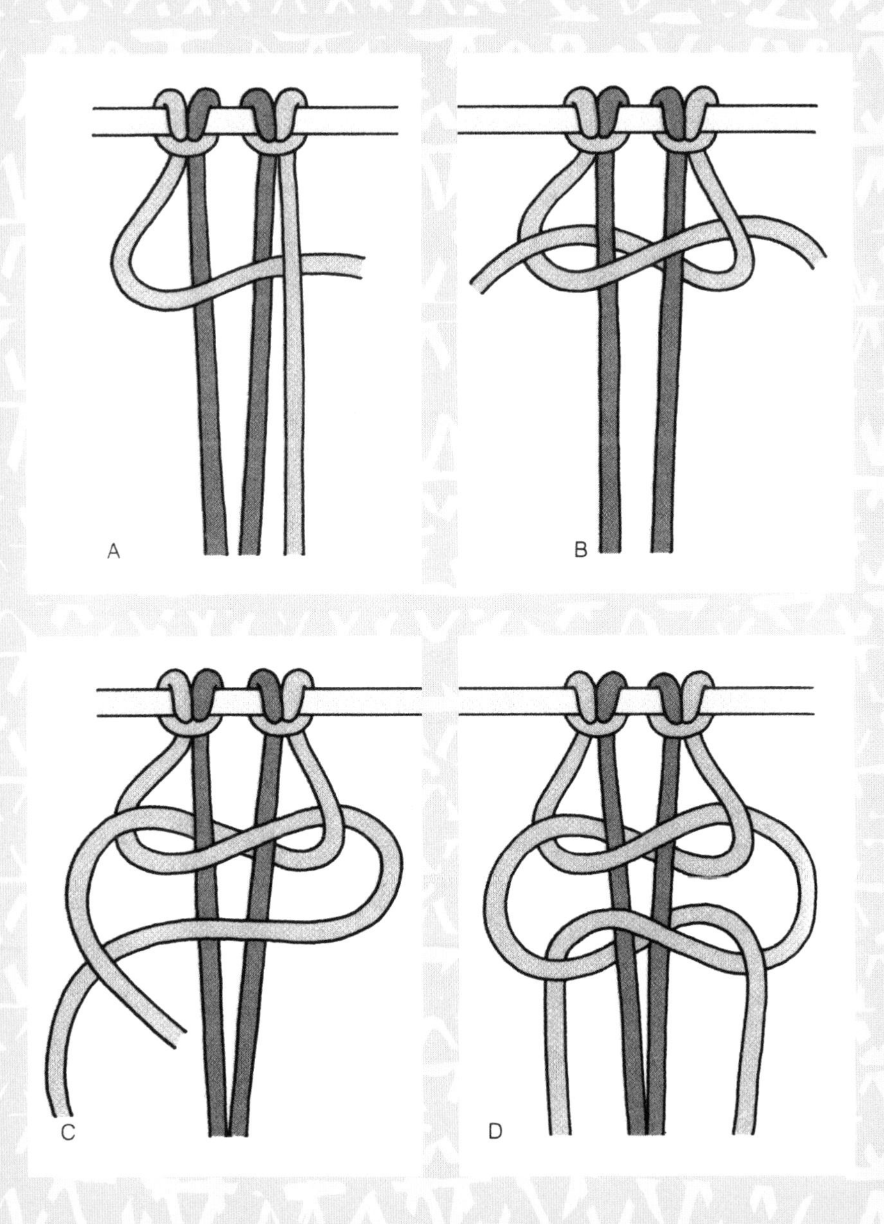

Loop knot

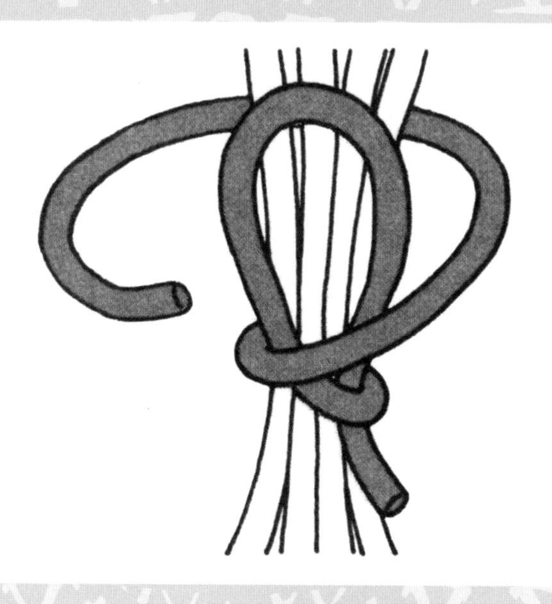

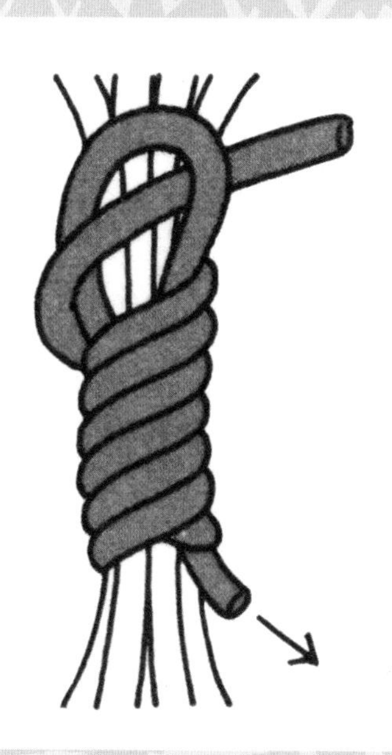

Step one

Get all eight pieces of long cord and feed them through your ring, making 16 lengths. Take one of the shorter pieces of cord and tie a loop knot about 2.5cm below the ring to secure them.

(Top tip: use a table leg, doorknob, or a toe to tie your ring to while you make the rest of your plant hanger!)

Step two

Divide your 16 pieces of cord into four groups of four. Take one group of four and tie eight square knots. Repeat this pattern with your remaining three groups of four.

Step three

Leave a 10cm gap, then tie a spiral knot on one of your groups. Continue with this spiral knot until you have a 10cm spiral! Repeat this with your remaining three groups.

Step four

Take two strands from the first group, and two from the second, then use these four strands to tie two square knots, leaving a 15cm gap after the spiral. Repeat this with the remaining strands, creating a diamond pattern with the knots. Repeat this whole step again after another 10cm gap, tying the original strands back together again.

Step five

Leave a 10cm gap, and use your last piece of shorter cord to tie a loop knot. Trim your pieces of string to create a nice neat tassel!

Decorate your plant hanger with dip dye, wrapping colourful wool around sections of it and attaching beads or pompoms!

Be more wonderfully weirdo

Creative thinking is about approaching a question or issue from a new angle. It's about coming up with a fresh interpretation of something and connecting ideas together in unexpected ways. It's thinking outside the box – no, it's throwing out the box entirely. By coming at a problem or idea from left-of-field, you're more likely to produce something exciting and never-before-seen. And new ideas are pretty much currency in today's world – aren't we all waiting for our next big idea?

Learning to think more creatively is for everyone – not just artists, writers, musicians and those who want to invent the next internet. As the world moves on, we need to learn how to think on our feet, to constantly adapt and to work in new ways. The world can feel like a big, scary, constantly evolving place – to keep our cool and sense of fun as we navigate our way through it, we need to adopt more creative, flexible ways of thinking as we head into the unknown.

There is one big, dominating trait that seems to link up many of the most creative people in the world: a desire to seek out new experiences. It makes sense: we all know that feeling when we go on holiday and feel our minds opening up to new ideas and ways of living. Suddenly we're off buying metal coffee pots for our hobs and deciding to definitely watch the sunrise every morning when we're back home, keen to bring some of that fresh 'holiday thinking' back with us into our daily lives. We are all creative beings at heart, but our workaday routines and obligations can often push aside that deep-rooted desire for trying new experiences.

Immersing yourself in different experiences from your norm can help your mind think differently. It activates new thought pathways and opens up creative channels. But here's the catch: in order to really benefit you have to *do* the activities, you can't just watch them from afar in a film, read about them or hear about someone else doing them.

Seeking out new experiences, people and unfamiliar locations provides us with a whole new set of references to draw on. By engaging in exciting new encounters, we are less likely to get stuck in the same thought patterns, too. We will become more open to change and spontaneity and as a result be less concerned when plans or ideas take an unexpected turn. We are less likely to approach life in the same old ways we always have, and with that, we're also less likely to employ the same old problem-solving methods and approaches to issues we're facing. You'll be less afraid of the unknown and more likely to take a few risks, knowing it will probably all be OK in the end, because it all worked out before, didn't it?

'Almost all creativity involves purposeful play.'
Abraham Maslow

Taking this idea of novelty a step or two further, another way to boost creative thinking seems to be to expose yourself to a bit of weirdness – reading Kafka was an example given in one study. After reading some such surreal stuff, people were more able to identify patterns in other material presented to them, linking up ideas where they may not have seen them before. It's thought that in trying to work out what the hell they had just read, their minds were super-active and wildly creative.

So, perhaps the answer to thinking more creatively, is to try lots of weird new things.

(See also see page 154 for more on mixing up your routines and breaking habits.)

Change it up

Anyone can welcome a bit of change into their daily lives. Generally, it's believed that simply doing a few activities that aren't part of our usual routine is enough to get those creative juices going and those new ideas flowing.

It's important to remember, though, that there is no one 'weird' fits all. After all, our own normal today would likely be lots of people's weirdness already, and certainly we'd almost all be considered weird to someone who visited us from 100 years ago. Be curious, never stop wanting to learn new things or to meet new people – if you feel like life has become a bit same-old, same-old, stop immediately and change direction – maybe literally. Be open to (almost) anything and creativity won't be far behind.

Brainstorm like Beyoncé

By the laws of averages, the more ideas you get down, the higher the chances are that one of them will be a good'un. Remember the sage advice that there's usually more than one solution to a problem? Try thinking about it from someone else's viewpoint and see what comes up. What would Beyoncé do? Or Bill Gates? What would your mum do? Write them all down and then focus on a few that ignite that fire in you.

Restrictions

It may sound as though it would produce the opposite results, but giving yourself a brief, a set of rules and a time limit can really help focus creative thinking. How many times have you felt overwhelmed and lost when asked to come up with an idea for 'anything'? Or left working on a personal project languishing for months because you didn't have a deadline?

Get out

An oldie but a goodie. Fresh air and exercise can do wonders for boosting creative thinking. While your body is busy moving, and with all that blood pumping to your ideas machine of a brain, you'll be surprised how many light-bulb moments you can generate. While you're out, try some of the ideas on pages 216–51 and see your neighbourhood with fresh eyes. (See page 220 for more on the power of movement and new ideas.)

Mood swings

Think about that poetry you wrote in the throes of first love, or the angry letters composed in your head when someone let you down. It's not always going to be the good stuff that gets produced, but creativity and our moods have some clear links, so next time you feel annoyed at your co-worker or are pumped after a dance class, put your thinking cap on, get out those paints or fire up your laptop and see what magic you can create!

Think surreal

J.P. Guilford's 'Unusual Uses Test' regularly crops up in studies and investigations into creativity the world over. This test of creativity involves coming up with as many non-traditional uses for a common object as you can – typically a brick, a newspaper or a cardboard box, but it could equally be a balloon, a bottle – or whatever item is currently languishing in the bottom of your bag. This easy test measures what Guilford called 'spontaneous flexibility', and his tests quickly became one of the main ways of testing creativity.

Suggested ideas for creative uses for a brick could be anything . . . You could use it to prop open a door, or as part of a game, you could throw it at someone from across the room . . . You could use it as a tiny chair. Ideas are then judged for their creativity and originality.

Test yourself here by coming up with 27 ideas for what you can do with an everyday object, like a paperclip. If you find yourself getting stuck, you can prompt yourself along by thinking of a random word and finding a link between the two. Paperclip + Tree? Paperclip Christmas tree decorations shaped like mini candy canes, anyone?

EXPERT IN PLAY

RUTH DUPRE, ARTIST AND TUTOR, CENTRAL ST MARTINS

Ruth Dupré was one of my favourite tutors at Central St Martins – she really helped me be playful with my creativity. Ruth is an award-winning artist working in many different media. She has exhibited widely nationally and internationally. She has taught at many institutions, including Central St Martins, Camberwell College of Art and The Royal College of Art.

I feel strongly that play is undervalued as a way of exploring ideas and educating ourselves. I have taught art for many years and have seen many of my students afraid to play – it requires confidence and courage. It is very exciting seeing people blossom once they allow themselves to play, and then to discover how to harness chance and the unpredictable in their work.

Interestingly, the best play is not free fall and anarchic, as many would expect. We all need boundaries and restrictions in every aspect of life, to feel secure and able to create. These restrictions can be as minimal as an instruction to draw with the left hand (or right, depending on the dominant hand). This simple instruction takes away responsibility for the result, it gives permission to play and experiment in a new way. It enhances creativity.

I have always been interested in how helpful these restrictions are to my students, and how extensively I should impose them. What level of instruction gives students permission to play but doesn't impinge on their ideas?

Control can quickly become a burden. It is important, and difficult, to give the right level of instruction to a group of students with different reactions to different tasks. We all need some degree of control. We all need to see merit in our results, and to develop confidence in our ability.

I will describe a painting project I run with these thoughts in mind, where I teach students how to paint a watercolour landscape or waterscape. Allowing the paint to be slightly out of control is difficult for some, but it is liberating. It is essentially playing. This short exercise demonstrates very clearly how rules can help in learning to accept play as a vital part of the process of creativity, how learning to use play productively is actually an important part of learning to be creative. In my own work I try to stay open and allow play to guide me. The only way I can describe that way of working is that it is like driving a car out of gear down an incline. I am still steering, I'm still driving, but I have relinquished control to gravity.

Watercolour sky

You will need

- A sheet of good-quality watercolour paper (good-quality materials are crucial to success)
- Largish watercolour brush
- Some watercolour paints

1

Paint a blue watercolour wash across the top two-thirds of the page. This ratio of one-third to two-thirds is a classical division of space, seen in painting, architecture, etc. It immediately gives a lift to the painting. Apply much more water than you would naturally, so the paint floods and bleeds in an uncontrollable way but begins to look like a sky with clouds and weather patterns.

2

Paint the lower section of the page with greens and tans (or blues, greens and greys for water), still using plenty of water and letting the pigment float around. Think about the horizon line, choose whether to put in hills or mountains. By this point, even a complete beginner can see that they have very quickly created a sense of space in their painting, so it looks like a readable landscape.

3

Splash a few strokes of another colour to merge into the blues, to suggest a sunrise or a storm cloud, etc. At this point decisions can be reversed, for example, paint can be lifted off the paper using a tissue, so experiment to get the effect you want. You can either leave the work to dry slightly, or continue working on the wet surface.

4

Choose whether to add suggestions of trees, bushes, animals, etc. (Look at Turner's very free landscapes and waterscapes for ideas.
With the confidence you have gained from the results so far, this next step will be much less daunting – if I had merely set the task without introducing the elements of play and unpredictability, I would have intimidated many of you by now!

Laugh your way to creative genius

Laughing is good for our health and as a happy by-product it can boost our creativity: if we're feeling playful, our ideas are more likely to be playful, too. In a brilliant study by the Massachussetts Institute of Technology into the relationship between improvisational comedy and creativity, titled 'Haha and aha!', those with a background in improv comedy were shown to be better at generating new product ideas than professional product designers!

The study was quick to acknowledge that there is a difference between wit and humour – humour being seen as something we are born with, whereas wit is the skill of making quick-thinking connections between concepts. Sound familiar? That's the very same skill needed to generate new creative ideas (see page 239). If you've ever been to an improv class, you'll know that the key lessons you're taught are how to think on your feet and how to make associations between different ideas as they arise. In their study, those who took part in an improv workshop increased their creative ideas output by 37 per cent.

So the good news is that these kinds of skills can be taught. And it's wholly possible to learn how to think more creatively. Even better: you can learn to think more creatively while having a good laugh.

For the most part improv comedy is a group activity and the aim is to make everyone look good – it's not just about you. So, it's a bit like a collective creative brainstorming session, but with all the extra funnies. The way to do this is to support each other, which is where the 'Yes, and . . .' rule of improv stems from. You take someone else's idea and build on it to create something new. 'I'm a banana!' 'Yes, and I'm going to peel you!', etc. You just have to go with it and do your best, and that's where the comedy magic happens (hopefully).

Boost your creative thinking with these Improv 101 exercises. Most involve a partner or a group of people, but you can try a few solo. If you're feeling truly inspired, check out your local improv group . . .

Yes, and . . .

The first rule of improv! Tell a story or act out a scene where every player starts their line with 'yes, and . . .'

. . . freeze!

One person is nominated the leader of the group and has to shout out random objects or concepts. Players have three seconds to physically form that idea – either individually or as a group.

Word ping pong

One player starts with a word, then the next player quickly says the first word they think of. Does everyone remember Mallet's Mallet? If you're flying solo, fill in these blanks with your own word associations:

Biscuit . . .
Lollipop . . .
Suitcase . . .
Robot . . .
Brazilian . . .
Mohican . . .
Flute . . .
Thorny . . .
Pillow . . .
Sponge . . .

TECHNOLOGY: THE DEATH OF CREATIVITY

Or so we were all led to believe would be the outcome. Well, actually it isn't true. Technology can open up creativity in new and exciting ways!

Those that criticise technology say it makes us lazy. There's an infinite online library of other people's ideas to copy. Moments of boredom in which great thoughts can flourish have been seriously reduced. And if we only ever look up the things we like and interact with our 'friends', we don't expose ourselves to differences of opinion that create a passionate debate and cause art that really *means* something. So say the anti-tech movement anyway.

Seeing what others do online can leave us feeling overwhelmed and intimidated; how are they so productive and successful and we're not?! And this thought spiral can prevent us getting started.

'Deep meaning lies often in childish play.'
Johann Friedrich von Schiller

BUT . . . It's *how* we use technology that matters. Used in a positive, life-enhancing way it can give us access to a universe of inspiration. Perhaps a little frighteningly, it's thought the average westerner is exposed to more ideas and information in just one day than our ancestors a few hundred years ago would have been in their entire lifetime. Through YouTube, anyone can learn a new skill – from how to draw a dog to how to apply drag queen makeup. Plenty of studies show those who play video games are more creative. And, yes, scrolling Instagram has many negatives, but it can also inspire you to create something amazing. You don't need anything more than a smartphone to take beautiful photos. Having access to these amazing ideas and tools means we all have the potential to be our most creative selves.

So how do we use technology to our advantage and not get lost in envy or a time vortex of videos of cats falling off sofas? First, there's some evidence to suggest that those cat videos aren't actually all that bad for us! As we know, a sense of humour can help us to think more creatively (see page 56) so if cats falling off sofas boost your mood, go for it! And memes are this generation's quick-witted language of satirical genius (or can be), so enjoy them for what they are and they might help spark an idea too.

Generally speaking, we all know when we are wasting time on the internet. There's a difference between 'being inspired' and aimlessly clicking on links. So the number one rule is to use technology as a meaningful platform to explore your curiosity. If you have the beginnings of an idea or a topic you are interested in, or if you're inspired by a particular style or creative outlet, get lost in that to your heart's content. You'll store up what you see and then, later, something will pop up as a new brilliant idea (maybe when you're lost in a daydream, see page 162). From Ted Talks to subject-specific websites on every topic under the sun (and beyond) there is plenty of information to pique your interest.

Technology also allows us to connect with people all around the world – a world that has shrunk in so many ways, but one where communities of like-minded creatives can form groups easily across continents. Whatever your niche, there'll be a group for you – or start one up yourself to exchange ideas and support.

The main message is to actually do something. Research and inspiration are great and encourage us to think more broadly and diversely. Without them, our ideas could end up stale or repetitive. But you still have to DO something with your creativity – you have to CREATE. So once you've finished your tutorial on how to achieve a good smoke effect in oil paints or how to sew crystals onto your jumper, make sure you then go and do it.

One other thing to bear in mind is that available content does not always equal good quality. More than 100 million photos and videos are uploaded to Instagram Every. Single. Day. Objectively, they can't all be the next David Bailey. So although technology allows everyone to express their creativity, it's sensible to curate what you see so you're not absorbing ideas that aren't useful for you. Don't just look at stuff you already know about and read articles by people you agree with, mix it up, allow things in your feed that you don't like, read articles by people who get your blood boiling. That's where passion and inspiration lie.

8 WAYS TO USE TECHNOLOGY TO BOOST CREATIVITY

1

Watch an online tutorial or lecture

Find a community of people doing the things that you want to do

Follow a few hashtags in your chosen subject to fill your feed with wonder

4

Start a Pinterest board on your topics that pique your interest

Allow yourself an hour to get lost on the internet – follow your curiosity link by link and see where you end up – fall down that internet rabbit hole

6

Find creative tools to enhance your skills – there are plenty of free demos around

Explore the create function on Instagram stories or draw on photos on WhatsApp pictures

Become a living-room DJ: make music with a free online app

EXPERT IN PLAY

KATE PHILLIPSON, ILLUSTRATOR, YOGA TEACHER, FOUNDER OF YOGA LIFE DRAWING

I noticed that the state of relaxed concentration I find in yoga is very similar to where I am when I'm drawing. I wanted to encourage people to use drawing to relax and have fun, but I recognised there was a lot of fear around it. People seemed to think you were either 'good at drawing' or not. And if not, you had no business giving it a go.

It's not surprising we feel this way – after your childhood scribbles, drawing is quickly taken away from you unless you choose to study art, which is often treated as a specialist subject, and with the weight of hundreds of years of art history behind it. It wasn't always like this. Drawing used to be like learning to read and write. Victorian children learned to draw as a matter of course, because in a world before computers (or even photography), draughtsmanship was a daily requirement, whether you were a dentist or a mapmaker. Some people may have gone on to become great artists, just as some people go on to use their writing skills to become authors or poets, but for most, being able to look at something and convey it to paper was a basic life skill. Now, people are bogged down in whether they are 'artistic' or not, and the idea of picking up a pencil terrifies them.

I started Yoga Life Drawing to give people a way into drawing. It was for people who would never in a million years go to a traditional Life Drawing class with a naked person in the middle of the room and two hours to draw one pose. Instead, it takes place in a yoga studio. We begin with a short 30-minute yoga class; we breathe and stretch and move together to relax. Then the yoga teacher becomes the model (fully clothed!). I give everyone paper, a board and some pencils – or pastels, felt-tips or paints for the adventurous – and we sit round on the floor. First we do super-quick poses – 30 seconds. You can't draw much in that time, so you simply have to get going, there is no time to think about it. The yoga teachers love this bit, as they can bust out their most acrobatic moves because they don't have to hold them too long! You'll only get a few lines down but drawing this quickly stops you overthinking. Then we'll do some 1-minute poses, then 2-minute, building up to 5-minute poses. We usually do some games, like draw with your 'wrong' hand, or without looking at the paper at all, or without taking your pencil off the paper. Then we'll do longer, up to 15-minute, poses.

All the time, I'm encouraging people to *look*. Drawing is much more about seeing than it is about mark-making. Really being able to look is becoming a lost art. When we go about our normal lives our brains make shortcuts for convenience. We see collections of shapes and our brain guesses 'face'. But if you draw a large circle with two circles for eyes, a 'nose shape' and a semicircle mouth, this will not look realistically like a face. When we really look, and shut down the shortcutting our brains want to do, we see that a face is full of other shapes entirely. When you begin to see these shapes, your drawings come to life.

Yoga Life Drawing is not about producing 'great art', it's to relax and find a flow state. Once you begin to properly look during the class, you learn a new skill to take out of the studio – how to see the world around you. Small things become interesting – the triangle of light on your coffee cup, the angles on a pile of magazines. The world becomes more fun, simply by actually looking at it. You CAN draw, we all can, it's just we DON'T draw. I am determined more and more of us will!

LIFE DRAWING

Life drawing doesn't have to be with naked people (although it can if you want it to!). Take it in turns to dress up in a costume, strike a pose (or see Yoga Life Drawing on the previous page!), then let your imagination run wild as you draw your friends, adding to how they look on the page. You can give them a crown, wings, eight legs – or maybe place them in an imaginary background of a rainforest or a wild, volcanic Martian terrain.

You are a creative genius!

We are all creative and we are all original. We just have to find our own unique way of expressing those qualities. Don't overthink it – just have fun being YOU, because your individual collection of experiences have made you into the amazing human being that you are today. There is no one else like you on the planet. We are born to be creative, and if you don't let out all that creativity stored away inside of you, you can start to feel stifled and frustrated in other areas of your life.

People who embrace their creativity are driven every day to get up and create – they don't find the time for being creative; they find time for everything else. It's what keeps them ALIVE. It really doesn't matter if no one ever sees any of your creative output or even if it's any 'good'

– that's not the point at all. With so much of our lives now uploaded to social media, it can sometimes seem as though unless it's on the internet, it doesn't count. Well, it definitely does. In fact, it's possibly even more powerful because a stronger, more personal and intimate connection can exist between you and what you create, instead of you producing something in order to please your expected audience, which can consciously or subconsciously influence your creative decisions. Stop worrying about what people think. Isn't that something we always want to tell our younger selves? Well, tell it to yourself now. Remember, when you were a kid and you just played and made things and they weren't very good, and your parents put your drawing up on the fridge anyway? Let's have more of that. Embrace your creative you!

How to celebrate being uniquely you

WWYD?

Spend a day doing exactly what you want to do – eat doughnuts for breakfast, wear an evening gown to the cinema, go to bed at 6pm and read comics under your duvet by torchlight. With every decision you make throughout the day, ask yourself what you really want to do. Not what other people want or expect you to do. (Tip: Don't try if you think you'll get fired at work, arrested or cause harm to someone else, obvs . . .)

Say thank you to yesterday you

Familiar with that feeling of waking up late, foggy-headed and regretting that extra glass of pinot noir? Don't let yourself hate yesterday you. Look after future you. Lay down the foundations for a positive, creative new you. And say thank you to yourself for that early night, pint glass of water, yoga class or the extra hour you spent prepping for the day today. Think about what will improve your life tomorrow and make the effort to do it today.

Find your medium

If you're not sure what kind of creative endeavour to bring into your life, write a really long list of lots of ideas for projects you think you might want to work on – like 50 or 100 or 563! Maybe you want to learn the dance routines to Lady Gaga or sew yourself a new dress. Maybe you want to make miniature models of your favourite pop band or life-size models of yourself – maybe you're yearning to craft a sprawling 6-foot sculpture called 'the inside of my mind' that takes over your entire living room? Maybe you want to write sci-fi fan fiction online or make a short film about honeybees. Keep going; among them there will be a sparkling gem that really gets you going and that you can't stop thinking about or wait to get started on. Then set yourself a deadline and do it. If you need an inspiration boost to get you started, have a browse on Pinterest or visit an art gallery and stroll around the permanent exhibits – identify what you connect with on a deeper, personal level. Really consider how they make you feel and what ideas they arouse in your beautifully creative mind.

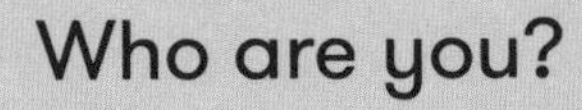

Who are you?

- 9 things that make you excited . . .
- 13 things that bring you joy . . .
- 7 things you need to stop giving a fuck about or let go of . . .
- 5 words that your best friend would use to describe you . . .
- 4 people who are important to you or who know you better than anyone else . . .

Stick, sprinkle, scribble: a self-portrait

Use this page to create a collage that represents the real you, then turn back to these pages whenever you need a reminder of your unique creative magic! Cut out pictures from magazines or draw an abstract self-portrait, then decorate it however you feel reveals the inner you in all its unique glory – sprinkle glitter, glue on sequins, write cartoon speech bubbles, sew or paint over the pages! Make these pages an expression of your inner thoughts and emotions – who you really feel like inside and not how you think you should present yourself. This is a glorious celebration of you, for you.

2

CONNECT

I'm a massive fan of organised fun, from back in the day at uni when friends would make games for our Friday night house parties. My favourite memory is of a blindfolded three-legged race on the pavement at 2am wearing some random items of fancy dress from the clobber box as a forfeit. I fitted myself into a six-year-old's *Monsters, Inc.* costume.

I know when someone pulls out some planned fun it can often feel contrived, but a huge heap of enthusiasm will make anything fun. Give it a chance – be a cheerleader! And if you're not feeling it, try to fake it until you make it. Ever tried fake laughing with a group for so long the laughter actually becomes real? (It's cringe-inducing, but – you can trust me on this one – it actually works.) Do you know why Christmas cracker jokes are all terrible? It's because it bonds the group together against the awful humour of the people who make the crackers. You share something. Organised fun is like that: the activity might be absolutely arbitrary, but it's the shared experience that makes it fun. In fact, we almost always find that the groups at Drink, Shop & Do that have the most fun do so not because they are having such a great time doing their awesome craft, but because the craft just kick-started a connection between the members of the group, bringing them together. They had to ask each other for help, they shared a laugh at their first attempts at making something, or they simply talked to someone new.

We might not know the meaning of life, but what brings life meaning for me is connection. Having deep, true, meaningful moments with people is what produces the strongest memories. My happiest, most contented times are when I understand someone and I am understood. That our brains' waves are dancing in perfect time with each other. For me, nothing is more special.

All mammals are social. We've needed each other since we survived together in tribes. And playing together, whether as children or as adults, is a no-pressure way of understanding how someone else thinks. We learn what their strengths and weaknesses are, and we find out and develop our own unique skills. We identify who we can trust and how to work together. Through play you learn the ways other people think and behave, so you can anticipate their reactions when it really matters. Living in the unknown can be anxiety-inducing, so feeling the security of being with another person – or group of people – that you know and trust is a relief. Playing builds trust. You test out your limits and values. You discover the boundaries of your relationship. Play is an attitude of openness and acceptance with each other, of judgements put to one side – because, after all, it's just a game.

When the circumstances have been set up for a playful approach to life in general we can let our guard down, let our truest self come forth, and when that's met with the same in return then you have those blissful moments of feeling in tune with the world around you. These moments are so important to nurture for our mental health. I went through a period in my mid-twenties where I had somehow surrounded myself with people who were a little uptight and not nurturing of their playfulness. And the disconnect I felt from the whole world was profound. It affected my every thought. Finding people who shared things that I found delightful enhanced the joy I took from those things because it meant creating a community to experience them with.

So be the person who encourages and makes a playful no-judgement space, so that other people in your life can let go and find the fun. What you give, you'll get back.

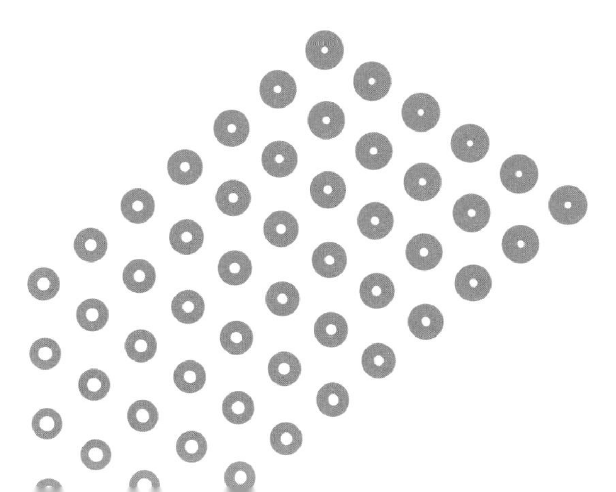

Doing a nice thing for someone is like a bit of modern-day magic. It makes the other person feel good and restores their faith in humanity – even if just for a few hours.

It reminds them that we're not all selfish idiots going about our day getting what we can from the world. And people who are having good days are more likely to do a nice thing for someone else. It creates a ripple effect of positivity and warm feelings. Grouching about on the Tube, passive-aggressively sighing when someone knocks into you doesn't make anyone feel life is scoring 10/10; it just makes you feel tired and annoyed. So spread some kindness, do some spontaneous good deeds and know that what goes around tends to come back around at some point. #whatgoesaroundcomesaround.

There's plenty of evidence that being more giving and acting altruistically makes us happier. And happier people are more relaxed, more fun to be around and more optimistic – which is all beneficial to living a more playful, creative life. It's a nice feeling knowing that you might have made someone's day a bit better.

Random Acts of Kindness

'Smile, it might never happen'

OK, so never, ever say that to anyone. But offering a smile to a stranger can be really reassuring. Everyone likes a friendly face.

Pay someone a compliment

If someone is wearing a nice outfit, looks like they are having a great hair day or you think they did something awesome at work – tell them! Think what a confidence boost it would give your day if someone said the same to you.

Words to inspire

If you've got some time on your hands, you could write little positive notes and leave them in unexpected places, like at bus stops, pinned to the noticeboard in your local café, or tucked inside library books. Keep those notes positive and brief, though – avoid creepy and stalkerish.

It's my round

Next time you're buying your morning double-shot almond-milk latte, pay for two coffees and give the person behind you a freebie.

Grant wishes

Make your own 'Take What You Need' posters (see over the page) and tape them to lamp posts, bins and bollards in your neighbourhood. Write your own inspiring affirmations or go all fortune cookie – 'you will be successful today' or '8 is your lucky number'. People can tear off whatever they need that day – and who knows, it might be what inspires them to make that change they've meant to for ages.

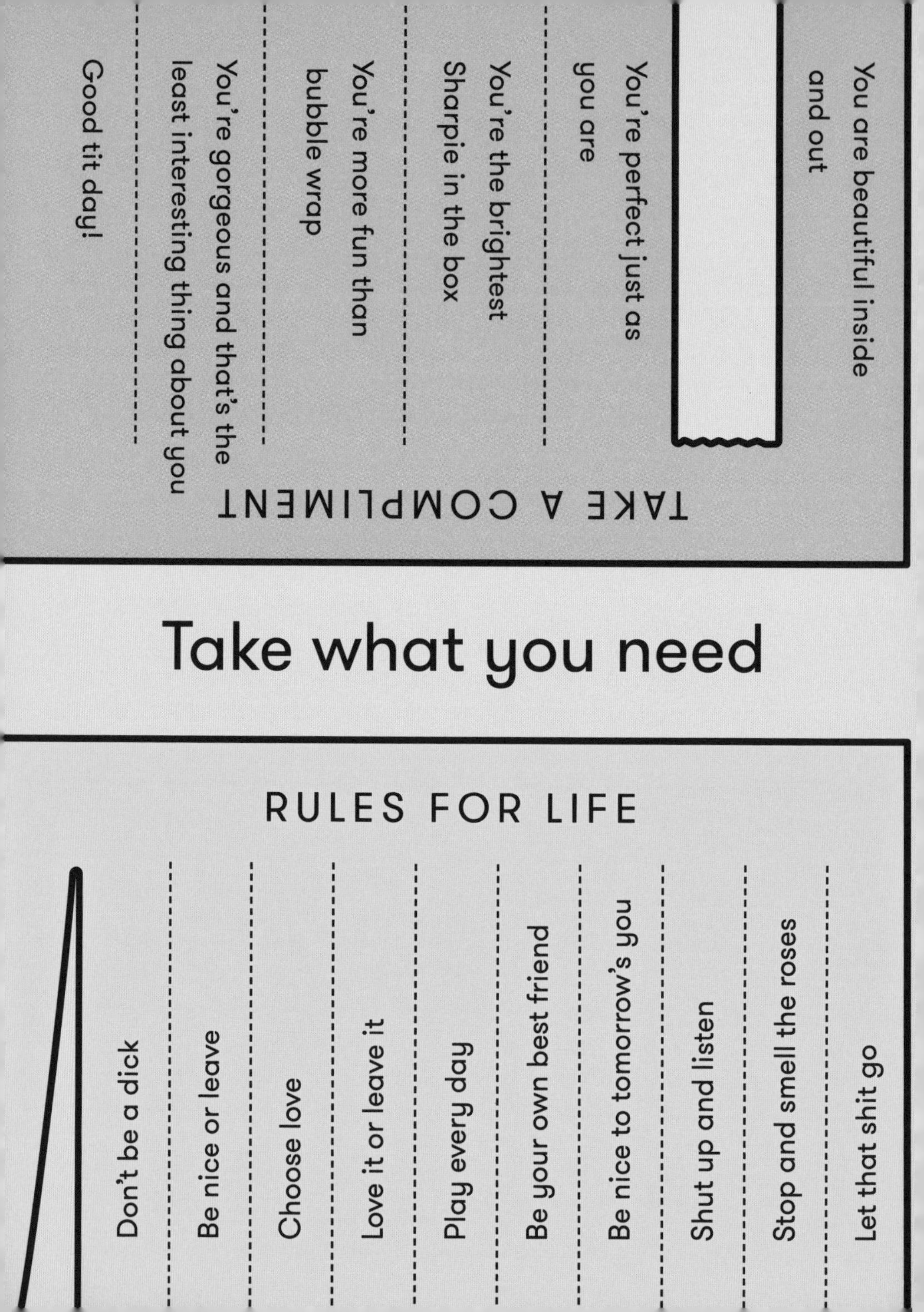

TAKE A COMPLIMENT
You are beautiful inside and out
You're perfect just as you are
You're the brightest Sharpie in the box
You're more fun than bubble wrap
You're gorgeous and that's the least interesting thing about you
Good tit day!
Take what you need
RULES FOR LIFE
Don't be a dick
Be nice or leave
Choose love
Love it or leave it
Play every day
Be your own best friend
Be nice to tomorrow's you
Shut up and listen
Stop and smell the roses
Let that shit go

Take what you need

MAKE A WISH

Sexy snog

Extra chocolate on your cappuccino

Cold hard cash

More dancing today

Laughter

Bubble bath

An extra hour in bed

Expensive champagne, please

A puppy to cuddle

Sweet FA – today I'm great

FORTUNE COOKIE

You'll have a mega mojo day

A friend is a present you give yourself

A hunch is creativity trying to tell you something

It can be done

Success is near

Curiosity kills boredom

Disbelief destroys the magic

Don't let ambition overshadow success

Connect with new people

If you think about it, you interact with more people on a regular basis than you realise. There's a sense of familiarity when you buy your milk from the same corner shop, swipe through at the station in front of the same staff, and pick up your lunch from the same sandwich shop.

You see these people more often than you see certain members of your family, so why not enrich those connections? It doesn't take

much to ask how they are, maybe find out their name, then each time you share a few words you'll learn a bit more about them. Make an effort to get to know your neighbours – take them a plate of biscuits or a casserole, Ramsay Street-style. The aim isn't to become their best friend, just to not be another silent, robotic stranger living a parallel life. Knowing there are people around you who you recognise, who recognise you and who you interact with, can make you feel more connected. You can watch out for each other, take their post in – plus having a quick chat is a great way to boost your mood. Hopefully this will also prevent you being one of those news stories where no one noticed you were dead in your apartment until three weeks later …

Maintaining a strong network of a few close friends has been shown time and again to have endless benefits for our happiness, self-esteem and even how long we live. The key, though, is that these friendships need to be solid – your thousands of Instagram or Twitter followers don't count, as those interactions are usually too superficial.

Anthropologist Robin Dunbar came up with a 'magic number' of 150 as the number of people humans can realistically hold in their social network. This is based on research into brain size and was backed up by looking at early hunter-gatherer societies, old English villages and even current Christmas card lists. Any more and it all starts to fall apart. But before you panic and realise you can count your actual friends on one hand, that's totally fine. Within that network of 150 are layers of connections – five loved ones, fifteen good friends, 50 friends and 150 meaningful contacts. (He also goes up to 1,500 people who you can name, but let's focus on the meaningful ones.)

As social media becomes more important in our lives and the nature of our interactions changes, these numbers may become skewed. But we still need a core group of like-minded folk. Close friends teach us about ourselves, they can challenge us and help us grow, support us when we need help, and we can model ourselves on their strengths. And, more importantly, they're fun to be around! How many times have you had a terrible day only to forget all about it after a night out with your best mates? Friends help us keep things in perspective.

Building your network

1

Don't just go to an event, make it work for you

Going to events, joining clubs and signing up for meet-ups doesn't necessarily connect you to other people. When you're there, you need to be brave and open up – ask a question, network, make eye contact. You need to be open and available – and smile! Start conversations. And think about launching your own events if there's nothing out there that interests you already. Nineteenth-century feminist literature book club with bespoke gin cocktails? We're in!

2

Ask for help or feedback

People love to help out and feel useful and most people are only too happy to share their expertise and experiences. So reach out to people who inspire, admire and interest you. Keep the dialogue going and then weave them into your network. Be useful back.

3

Start online

Find like-minded people near you through your online networks and then when you're ready, move it to a face-to-face meet-up. Maybe even share something you've made from this book on Instagram with the hashtag #getyourplayon. You can then make a new buddy bonding over your paper cactus pictures.

4

Join a team

For a ready-made gang, starting or joining a team is an instant way to create a regular group of new pals. It could be a sports team, five times champions Quiz Team Aguilera or any other team-based activity you fancy.

MAPPING OUT YOUR CONNECTIONS

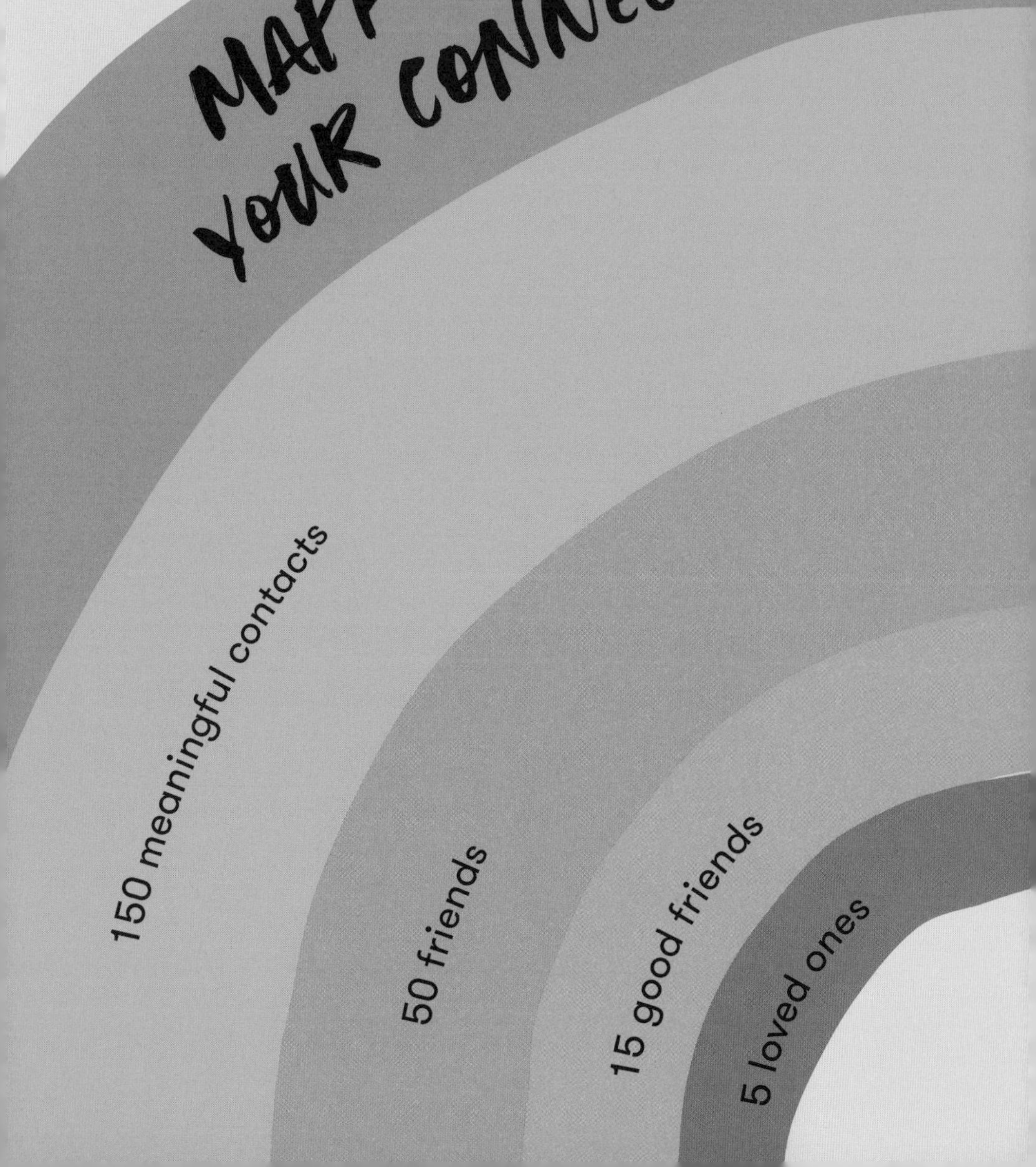

150 meaningful contacts

50 friends

15 good friends

5 loved ones

Write out or draw in your network of connections, based on Robin Dunbar's magic number of 150. You'll probably see your network is larger than you think. If you're feeling particularly full of love, why not send a card to everyone on your connections list to let them know you're thinking of them.

EXPERT IN PLAY

KIM LEADBEATER MBE
THE JO COX FOUNDATION

The Jo Cox Foundation was established by the friends and family of the late Jo Cox MP to create something positive from the tragedy that was her murder. Kim Leadbeater MBE is Jo's sister and the foundation's ambassador.

Play to connect

Under normal circumstances most of us probably give little thought to the importance of 'human connection'. We just get on with our lives. Those of us lucky enough to be surrounded by friends, family and loved ones look forward to spending time with them, sharing a meal, having a laugh, or just chatting about whatever is going on in our lives. If we are in work, we engage with colleagues. In our spare time we might meet up with people who share an interest, or through sport, clubs, schools or places of worship. In all those ways we are engaging in the kind of connections that can unite, inspire and support us in good times as well as bad, but we are often quite oblivious to the impact they are having on our health and wellbeing and quality of our lives.

The Covid pandemic brought the importance of connection into sharp focus. Tragically, for many people coronavirus meant the loss of loved ones, and, sadly, for all of us it also meant the loss of many freedoms and interactions with other humans. I suspect for lots of people it was only when they were told they couldn't do all those things that they became conscious of how important they were. It's a cliché, but it's true that 'you don't know what you've got until it's gone'. Forced by the health crisis into varying degrees of isolation, we stopped taking it for granted that we could go to the pub, gym, church, or meet other parents at the school gate. We came to appreciate that connecting with others was not just something we do, it was crucial to our physical and mental wellbeing.

I really hope that after all the pain and loss and trauma, one good thing to come out of the pandemic is that many more of us have learned the value of connection, of community and of good old-fashioned neighbourliness.

Since the murder of my sister, Jo Cox MP, in 2016, much of my time has been taken up with working at the Jo Cox Foundation, the charity we set up in her name, to build strong, compassionate communities and to bring people together; building on the work Jo had started on loneliness and social isolation and addressing some of the divisions our country has seen in recent years.

We run The Great Get Together campaign – a national platform for people to organise events, large and small, to bring people together in their communities; we have worked hard to develop the 'More in Common' network of volunteer groups across the UK, focusing on the power of human connection and togetherness, and during the pandemic we set up the 'Connection Coalition', a cross-sector network of organisations, charities, companies and groups united in our belief that we can build a better future for everyone by building strong relationships and connected communities. More and more work of this kind has been going on around the country. Connections have been formed that will be invaluable in the future.

Despite much of this work being new to me, my background in physical activity, health and wellbeing, along with my time working in education, have meant that I have been able to continue my lifelong passion for working with people and communities to facilitate positive health and wellbeing outcomes. All inspired by my sister and our shared belief in the best of humanity and the power of human connection.

But while we address some very serious issues through the work of Jo's foundation, we also try to keep 'fun' at the heart of much of what we do – partly because this makes our work so much more engaging and partly because I know my sister would expect nothing less.

Indeed, Jo and I were blessed with a childhood full of fun, and 'play' was integral to this. As kids, we would play on our BMX bikes, go roller-skating, climb trees, build dens and invent dance routines. Mum and Dad would take us to parks and the seaside and we would spend hours with family and friends playing games – indoors and outdoors. We both played sport at school and I still play hockey; the sense of companionship and togetherness that being part of a team generates is powerful and also encapsulates a true 'more in common' spirit; a bunch of people brought together and united by a shared passion, irrespective of their differences. And whether it is playing hockey on the pitch, cards in the pub afterwards or badminton and board games on a weekend away, the camaraderie and connection is compelling.

When Jo went to university we missed each other terribly. It was probably the first time either of us learned the meaning of loneliness. But I kept up with my hockey and Jo made new friends and new connections, and found new ways to channel her inner need for play.

When Jo had children, things changed again, and massively for the better, of course. Jo was a truly inspirational mum who spent hours playing with her children. They love the outdoors too and they climb trees with as much excitement as we ever did. The joy of hearing them laugh and scream as they run around the woods or the park is infectious, and I for one am in no hurry to see them grow out of it – I hope they never do! I have taken my role as 'crazy auntie' very seriously – teaching them games new and old. And when we take them on the train from Yorkshire to London they play dominoes, cards and I-spy with Grandma and Grandad and we read books and do colouring together. I'm genuinely not sure who enjoys it the most!

I believe that whatever life throws at you, you have to do the best you can to stay positive and to keep the pleasure of play alive. After Jo's murder that was incredibly tough, and it still isn't easy. Working for her foundation has helped – particularly seeing the pleasure we have brought to so many people through the fun of The Great Get Together, the Run for Jo, The Jo Cox Way bike ride and many more events.

Lockdown forced us to rethink how we did things, but with a bit of creativity we kept the show on the road. We couldn't cycle or run in a group, so we did it wherever we were in the world and shared our stories and pictures to keep the sense of togetherness strong. Online craft sessions and virtual discos took the place of get-togethers on village greens and town squares. As a family we did quizzes, fancy dress and charades, all in the safety of our own homes but very much 'together'.

By having to be creative in this way, we confronted head on the need to stay connected. It's my hope, and my belief, that when we look back on Covid as a nightmare in the past we will also remember the lessons we learned. Not to take connection for granted. Never to forget how hard some people work to keep our communities safe and well. No longer to put out of our minds the thought that somebody down the street might be desperate for a bit of company or just a smiling face.

For me, the work I have been involved with – both nationally and locally – since Jo was killed has kept me going. Human connection is important in this, personally and professionally. But we need to take a holistic approach – addressing physical, mental and social wellbeing, if we are to meet Jo's challenge that this should never be a country 'where thousands of people are living lonely lives forgotten by the rest of us'.

In the most terrible of circumstances we have come to understand and appreciate the importance of connection. We have an opportunity now to embed that understanding in how we build a stronger, happier and more united country going forward. Play has an important role in this – it binds us in a unique way, through sport and exercise, arts and crafts, indoor and outdoor games or on a trip to the land of make-believe – where Jo and I spent much of our childhood together.

Organised fun – why we love games and have done for millennia

People tend to think organised fun is the sad cousin of 'real' fun. Fun is supposed to happen spontaneously, isn't it? You shouldn't have to plan how, where and when you'll be having fun and let everyone know in advance and chase up their RSVP. Isn't organised fun just the horrible bit of a corporate bonding trip before everyone heads to the bar?

Right, now that you've got over yourself, let's see how organised fun can actually be a whole lot of good times. People have been playing structured games – the most basic form of organised fun before the advent of the stag do – for thousands of years. The oldest board game we know of is around 5,000 years old and belonged to those clever Ancient Egyptians. Sadly, someone not quite so clever let the side down and forgot to put the rules back in the box, so we're not sure how to play it. Dice have been around for millennia, too – a set of 3,000-year-old dice was found in Iran, and the Romans loved a bit of dice (and wine) of an evening (probably). They weren't just used in gaming and gambling, the Romans loved a bit of fortune-telling with dice too – with higher numbers signalling good luck. In England, a game called Hazard stuck around for 500 years, from the fourteenth century. It was a complicated dice game that eventually got simplified and turned into craps, which is still played today, especially in America. Mostly dice are used in games of chance, but games of skill like chess and Go have also been played for over 1,000 years. The history of cards is a bit patchy, but it is thought that card games made their debut around the ninth century, originating in the East and travelling to Europe via Egypt. Back then cards looked more like tarot cards, depicted with elaborate symbols of goblets, coins, polo sticks and swords. We can thank the French for the four decks on modern card tables, who came up with this enduring design around 1480.

Today, there are literally tens of thousands of games to choose from – and many have broken ranks and escaped the games table. They are often beautifully designed and illustrated – artworks in their own right – and gaming cafés are springing up in every town. From snooker to Dungeons and Dragons, playing games is a perfect way to spend time with the people you love. Or with people you don't know that well. Yet.

To paraphrase the wise words of Plato, through playing games you learn about people's characters. Weighted dice were found in the ruins of Pompeii, so even back then, game-playing brought out the worst in people. And we all know that person who steals money from the bank in Monopoly. But games can also bring out our fun-loving side, decrease stress and help bond people as we talk, laugh and challenge each other. That's one reason it's thought board games have remained popular – even *gained* popularity – despite the sophistication of online gaming. Games are inherently a social experience, which bring huge benefits to our mood and wellbeing. If a game is silly or embarrassing, or makes you look ridiculous, you can unite *against* the game! Playing games can also teach us to take risks and boost self-confidence, especially if there are some challenging forfeits involved . . .

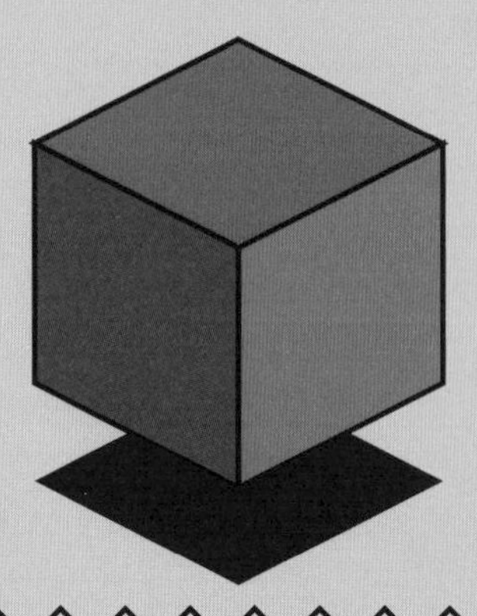

Good ol' pass the parcel

Yes, it's lots of work to prep this one, but everyone knows what they are doing with it and you can get music on that everyone will have a dance to. It also opens up smaller groups to work as one big team together, which is great if not everyone knows each other.

Tips: Make the present pretty and high effort so it doesn't feel kiddy. Even if it's a big group, only do eight layers – you don't need to make a layer for everyone like at a kids' party. Make the last layer a distinctive wrapping if you need/want the prize to go to a certain person.

You will need

- A prize. How about an inflatable guitar or a tinsel wig?
- Wrapping papers, scissors and tape.
- Sweets, or if you're a healthy lot, maybe some free sample toiletries?
- A noise maker or ability to stop the music.
- Modelling balloons and pump.
- Crackers.
- Limbo stick – AKA a broom or a string.

How it's done

Guests pass the parcel around until the games master sounds their noisemaker or turns off the music, if you're at home. They then unwrap a layer to find either a prize (sweets), an avalanche of paper confetti or a forfeit. When it gets to the last layer, play a banging tune to get everyone dancing with an air guitar.

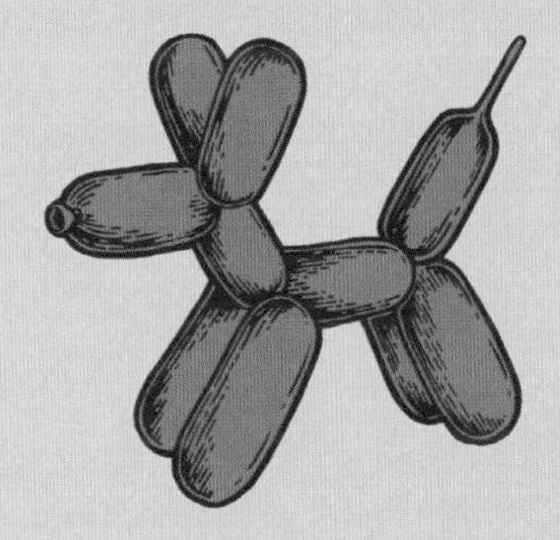

FORFEIT: Make a balloon animal and ask your group to guess what it is as you form it. Keep adding to it until they get it right!

FORFEIT: Eat a cracker, then whistle until the team guess the song. Try 'Working 9-5' or 'the Macarena' or just 'Happy Birthday'.

FORFEIT: Read out the last text message that you received.

FORFEIT: Shimmy under a limbo stick.

FORFEIT: Give your group a rendition of 'Single Ladies' in your finest Beyoncé voice.

FORFEIT: Silently enact an animal until any person guesses it.

FORFEIT: Recite the alphabet backwards in 20 seconds.

FORFEIT: Pour a cup of ice water over your head.

FORFEIT: For the next 15 minutes you must only sing whatever you want to say to the tune of happy birthday.

FORFEIT: Spend the rest of the game blindfolded.

Confessions

You will need

- Pens.
- Paper.
- A hat.
- A box of chocolates.
- Guests with full glasses.

How it's done

Guests pass around pieces of paper and each write a secret or fact about themselves that no one at the table knows. They then fold it up and place it in the hat. Take it in turns to read each one aloud. Guests have to guess who the secret/fact belongs to. If they guess correctly, they get a point. If they guess incorrectly, they have to take a forfeit (see opposite for forfeit inspiration).

I got in trouble with the police when…

The meanest thing I did at school was…

I actually got physically violent when…

The nasty thing I did to my sibling was…

On the wildest night of my life I…

I was having a surreal hangover, then…

My most daring sexual encounter was the time…

My nearest death experience…

I've broken the law by…

At a festival I ended up…

Forfeits

FORFEIT: Show everyone your best twerk.

FORFEIT: Smell the feet of everyone in the room and rank the top three and worst three.

FORFEIT: Think of five words that rhyme with your own name and make them into a rap.

FORFEIT: Name five parts of the body each spelled with only three letters.

FORFEIT: Go outside and walk 50 metres of pavement like a model on a catwalk.

FORFEIT: Draw a face on your hand and only use it as your ventriloquised dummy for the rest of the game.

FORFEIT: Do not read this out: do a cat impression until someone shouts 'pussy'.

FORFEIT: High-five everyone in the room.

FORFEIT: Spend half an hour tied to the person whose birthday is closest to your own.

FORFEIT: Give one piece of advice to everyone in the group.

Not just culture; all other pops included.

You will need

2 players or 2 teams.
A homemade scoreboard with counters or a scorecard.

How it's done

First to toot the imaginary horn (as in make a loud noise of your choice and 'honk the air'/ stick your hand up/press the table) gets to answer. If they answer correctly, move forward on the score board; if they answer incorrectly they have to do a forfeit. First to get ten questions right wins.

Which BBC show started in 1964 with star performances, including one from Dusty Springfield?

Top of the Pops

Which runner-up in *Pop Idol* 2002 had a hit with 'Anyone of Us (Stupid Mistake)'?

Gareth Gates

Which TV Pop had a penchant for donuts?

Homer Simpson

Which nu metal band had an album track called 'Pop a Pill' in 2010? (Their name happens to sound like the popped maize snack.)

KoЯn

What style of shirt famously uses clothes poppers?

Cowboy/Western

Which legendary band did a Rice Krispies jingle in 1964?

The Rolling Stones

Which monkey started selling us breakfast cereal in 1985?

The Coco Pops monkey

In French what replaces the slogan 'Snap! Crackle! Pop!'?

Cric! Crac! Croc!

Which breakfast brand had a 3,200-foot Times Square store in 2010?

Pop Tarts

Which brand of lollipops has a logo designed by Salvador Dali?

Chupa Chups

What 'pop' is a single portion of fruit-flavoured ice on a stick known as?

Popsicle

Which company owns the Pop Tarts brand?

Kellogg's

What gas is in fizzy pop?

Carbon dioxide

How high can a corn kernel jump when it pops?

About 90cm

What year did popcorn start being sold in movie theatres?

1912

What candy contains pressurised carbon dioxide gas bubbles?

Popping candy

What was the chemist who developed popping candy trying to make at the time?

An instant soft drink

Which legend of the 80's NY pop-art scene featured colourful outlined figures and a barking dog in his work?

Keith Haring

'Crying Girl' is a famous piece by which pop-art artist?

Roy Lichtenstein

What brand of soup featured in Andy Warhol's pop art?

Campbell's

In which decade was Popeye the sailor man created?

1920s

Spell Popeye's wife's name.

Olive Oyl

What does Popeye eat for strength?

Spinach

From which flowering plant does opium come?

Poppy

What is a thin nylon sock called?

Pop sock

At what age did stars like Kurt Cobain and Amy Winehouse pop their clogs – said to cause a spike to join 'the club'?

27

What animal goes pop in the children's rhyme?

The weasel

What does the K in K-pop stand for?

Korean

Which fictional nanny insists that she must have the second Tuesday of the month off?

Mary Poppins

Let's celebrate!

Sometimes we end up seeing the people we care about only a couple of times a year at someone's birthday drinks. Or a dinner gets cancelled because of working late, then it gets moved again for some other lame reason, then suddenly it's been six months since you've seen the people who bring joy and meaning to your life. Stop waiting.

And stop making excuses. We've all learned the hard way that life is too short to delay, to hold out for that perfect moment when you can be happy, or that special occasion when you crack open the bottle of champagne in your fridge that you got last Christmas. Start celebrating everything. Wear your favourite dress or suit today, because you look frickin' awesome in it and feel like a boss. Eat pizza off your grandma's best china – you'll be enjoying it and getting use from it in a way that you wouldn't if you kept it in the cupboard for special. Yes, you might break a plate, and you'll need to replace your fancy shoes sooner, but how much fun will you have had?

Literally every day is an national day of something fun – so let's get celebrating some of them. Celebrate all of them! And that's not even factoring in time to properly get involved with the main holidays of the year. Celebrate the equinox, celebrate the last in the series of your favourite TV show with a themed night, celebrate it being the first snow of the year or the fact that you've finally finished painting the hallway. Make time to treat yourself, to acknowledge that just being alive is a really special honour and that every day should be welcomed with open arms and grabbed hold of! Shrug off that bad day at work, get the gang together and honour it in the only way it should be honoured. Here are some of the very best national days for your calendar now:

YEARLY CALENDAR

JAN	1st National Bloody Mary/Hangover Day	8th Elvis Presley's Birthday	14th Dress Up Your Pet Day	21st Squirrel Appreciation Day
FEB	1st Saturday Ice Cream for Breakfast Day	5th Shower with a Friend Day	17th Random Acts of Kindness Day	26th Tell a Fairy Tale Day
MAR	1st Peanut Butter Lover's Day	13th Open an Umbrella Indoors Day	21st National French Bread Day	31st Crayon Day
APR	2nd National Ferret Day	13th National Scrabble Day	14th National Dolphin Day	27th National Tell a Story Day
MAY	4th National *Star Wars* Day	16th National Sea Monkey Day	22nd World Goth Day	31st National Macaroon Day
JUN	9th National Donald Duck Day	14th National Bourbon Day	21st National Selfie Day	25th Take Your Dog to Work Day
JUL	7th Dive Bar Day	10th Pina Colada Day	29th Lipstick Day	31st Avocado Day
AUG	12th Middle Child Day	13th Prosecco Day	16th Rum Day	19th International Bow Day
SEP	5th National Be Late For Something Day	14th **National Cream Filled Donut Day**	15th National Cheese Toast Day	25th National One-Hit Wonder Day
OCT	1st Friday World Smile Day	13th National No Bra Day & Yorkshire Pudding Day	26th Pumpkin Carving Day	29th National Hermit Day
NOV	12th Ryan Gosling's Birthday	13th World Kindness Day	19th National Play Monopoly Day	28th National French Toast Day
DEC	8th Pretend to Be a Time Traveller Day	12th Poinsettia Day	21st Crossword Puzzle Day	31st Champagne Day

The lost art of letter writing

How many great stories start with a letter? A passion-fuelled love letter, kissed all over, ink smudged with tears of yearning; a stack of correspondence bound up in faded ribbon found stashed under a squeaky floorboard, revealing secrets and a whole life; friendships struck up, back and forth over years; missives from the front in wartime, captured forever in history.

Ever since you sent off for that free toy on the side of your cereal box, it's hard to beat the thrill of receiving post. It's easy to fire off an email or send a quick text while you're waiting for the bus – and these all play their role in helping us feel connected – but there's nothing quite like the pleasure and intimacy of a handwritten letter. Knowing that someone has taken the time to sit down with only you in their minds to pen their thoughts makes you feel loved. Letters are reflective, capturing the richer details of a moment, and can be cherished, to be rediscovered and laughed or cried at decades later.

Spending time writing and thinking about people you care about is a great mood-booster for you too. There's a load of research into the benefits of handwriting over keyboard action. Writing by hand activates different areas of the brain, can help you remember things better, can enhance cognitive function and develop fine motor skills. Writing by hand is also thought to encourage creative thinking. Finally, writing letters will improve your handwriting – there's nothing more off-putting or less authoritative than an adult with the indecipherable scrawl of an infant.

Top tips for letter writing

- Letters are perfect for reaching out to people you don't know; they can make a great first impression. Send them to your neighbours to introduce yourself or write to people you admire and tell them why they inspire you. Style it up and stand out. Use good-quality paper and a proper ink pen, and write in joined-up writing, not capital letters (like a serial killer).
- Write a letter to your future self and keep it to read in two, five, ten years' time. Or write a letter to your past self, telling them how proud you are of them and it's all going to be OK. Or write a letter to yourself *now*, from either your past or future self, with wise words of advice and a resounding, uplifting pep talk with hindsight.
- When you write your letters, celebrate the difference between digital and physical. Illustrate your words to add detail, make notes and decorate the margins. Include little extras you know will brighten the recipient's day. Make your letters a visual experience, more exciting and personalised than bland sans serif on a bright screen.
- Write key words in a different font to emphasise your point – see overleaf for some ideas.
- Add confetti to the envelope for a special (annoying) treat.
- Decorate the envelope, or make your own out of pretty paper – leave enough space to clearly write the address.

Take inspiration from the wonderful talent moludesigns.com to make a handwritten note to send to a friend. Add your own font flourishes and decoration from the inspiration here.

A QUICK
NOTE
to say
YOU ARE
Awesome

EXPERT IN PLAY

JONATHAN CRANSTON
THE TRAVELLING VET

Animals at play

Do animals play? Just take a stroll through the English countryside on a warm spring day and the evidence is clear. The lamb frolicking over the lush spring grass, the bullock bounding around a barn of freshly bedded straw, or the young colt turned out onto a lush pasture, bucking and kicking as he gallops in delight.

Why do animals play? In many cases it is an instinctive necessity, an evolutionary tool to develop and perfect social, physical and cognitive skills, which are imperative to their very survival. The lion cub stalking and pouncing on an unsuspecting butterfly as it flutters across the savannah, the wolf pups writhing and rolling with each other in the thick prairie grass, or the wildebeest calves dodging, weaving and cantering as they trail each other through the grazing herd on the open plains of the Serengeti.

But sometimes, many times, animals will simply play for the pure enjoyment and gratification of it. No explanation, no evolutionary advance, no survival instinct, just for the pleasure and fun of it. The dolphin ducking and diving as it surfs in a ship's wake. The chimpanzees scampering and scurrying in pursuit of each other through the maze of decaying detritus on the forest floor. The Nuthatch as it acrobatically zigzags in and out of the hedgerow, or the polar bears wrangling and wrestling in the snowy Arctic tundra, simply playing for playing's sake.

And to glimpse such behaviours in the animal kingdom is to peek into their private world, to see behind nature's veiled curtain, for it is only when fear is absent and trust is established that play emerges. Then you know you have truly encountered nature.

Connect with the animal within

1

Entertain yourself by dressing to camouflage with your sofa. Play 'Karma Chameleon' when guests arrive.

2

Next time you hand your loved one something, why not start a friendly and unspoken game of tug like a puppy?

3

Get horsing around. Take a little gallop and leap over that puddle.

4

Make a little magpie collection of pictures of things you love.

5

Play fight, take a boxercise class or maybe arm-wrestle a friend.

Play with your food

So many of our celebrations revolve around food in some way. Happy memories of childhood birthday parties with cocktail sausages on sticks and mini pizzas, boozy late-night dinners with friends, long lunches that roll into evening meals on holiday . . . not forgetting the family arguments and sulks around the Christmas dinner table.

However, a fairly embarrassing – but not exactly surprising – number of us now regularly eat our meals in front of the TV. According to a royal biographer, even The Queen does it! And a separate dining room is no longer considered an essential when buying a new house. Since more and more of us live in flats, there's not really space for a dining room in our lives. We're more likely to eat out, on the run, order in and snack, scoff and multi-task while we flick between screens.

Despite all this, 49 per cent of us still think sharing a meal together is one of the best ways to spend proper time with each other, and we wish we were doing it more often. It slows us down. We have time to check in with our loved ones. We can ask questions, discuss our days and try to figure out what the hell is happening in the world. We can find a little patch of security in our otherwise topsy-turvy existence. It offers a break away from the constant input of digital information, and a chance to actually connect with people. A home-cooked meal is more likely to be healthier too.

It doesn't have to be a full-on feast, though – a randomly assembled picnic in the park can be way more fun than a fancy spread. And who doesn't love to play with their food? Food that is interactive, where you build and dip and assemble and then go back for more. Sharing plates around the table brings people together much more than a single plate we keep to ourselves! Meals are all the better when you're getting involved in them: think a table overflowing with takeaway boxes, Spanish tapas, Middle Eastern mezze – small plates to divvy up between friends and fight over the last falafel ball.

Pick any night of the week and just get people round, no pressure – Waffles for Dinner Wednesday? Light a few candles, stick on some appropriate music – hey – dress up and have theme night! Play games and drink cheap wine. Your table doesn't have to be big, or even a proper table – just somewhere you can sit and spend time together. Don't limit yourself to staying at home either. Embrace traditions from warmer spots in the world and gather in squares and public spaces and eat together – it's all about community. However you do it, gather your nearest and dearest to break bread – or in this case you can construct tacos!

Bonus bonding activity

Put all your phones in the middle of the table. No one can look at them until the end of the meal. The first one to crack has do the washing-up.

TACO

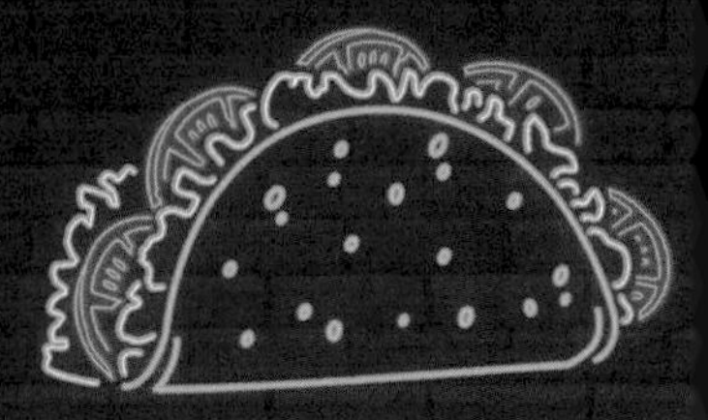

Epic buffalo cauliflower tacos with pink pickled onions, pico de gallo salsa and vegan sour cream by @ILoveSayCheese

Make 16 tacos

- 2 heads of cauliflowers
- 200g pineapple (fresh or tinned)
- 5 plum tomatoes, diced
- Big squeeze of agave syrup
- 2 tbsp lime juice
- 500ml apple cider vinegar
- 150g caster sugar
- 2 large red onions, very thinly sliced
- Vegetable oil, for frying
- 400g plain flour
- 100g cornflour
- 2 tbsp smoked paprika
- 2 tbsp sriracha hot sauce, plus extra to serve
- 1 litre sparkling water
- 16 corn tacos
- Handful of micro coriander
- Vegan sour cream, to serve

1. Cut the cauliflower into very small florets (save the stalk and leaves to make stock).
2. Peel and dice the pineapple (or drain if using tinned), then mix with the diced tomatoes in a small bowl and add the agave syrup and lime juice.
3. Heat the vinegar and sugar in a small pan over a medium heat until the sugar dissolves (about 5 minutes). Remove from the heat and

allow to cool slightly, then add the sliced red onion and leave to pickle for 30 minutes. You can decant into a clean jar after 30 minutes or leave in the pickle juice and place in the fridge.

4. Pour the oil into a large heavy-based pan and place over a medium-high heat – the amount of oil needed will depend on the size of your pan.
5. Mix together the flour, cornflour, paprika and sriracha, then slowly add the sparkling water (you might not need all of it; you want the batter to be the consistency of double cream). Dip each piece of cauliflower in the batter.
6. To test if your oil is hot enough, dip a spoon into your batter and let a drop from the spoon hit the oil. If it rises to the top instantly it's ready; otherwise keep testing.
7. When your oil is ready carefully add the cauliflower to it. You'll need to do this in batches, giving your cauliflower space so that it doesn't all stick together. It should take a couple of minutes (maximum) per batch; watch it constantly and remove the cauliflower once it turns golden brown and crispy. Drain on kitchen paper, then place in a bowl covered with foil to keep warm.
8. Put the tacos into a screaming hot frying pan (do not add oil), again in batches so each one has enough space. It will take 30 seconds to 1 minute on each side to heat up. When each taco is ready, wrap in a clean tea towel to keep steaming hot while you heat the rest.
9. Phew! That's it! All hands on deck as you grab a taco and load up on toppings, garnishing with micro coriander and drizzling with hot sauce and sour cream.

3

IMAGINE

When I'm not feeling playful, I find it so hard to be imaginative. In fact, if I find I'm not getting lost in an imagined world on a regular basis, that's a little telltale sign for me that I've not planned in enough downtime to rest, recharge and play.

I'm at my most imaginative when I have a huge, far-off dream I want to aim for (or just the very beginnings of an idea) and then I start to fill in the details that will get me there. Allowing myself to imagine a different situation or set of circumstances has made so many things a reality for me. Imagination is the first – and I think the most important – step towards a new way of doing things.

Imaginative play can help us understand how other people feel. It can help us empathise and relate to those around us. It can boost our mood and lift us out of a rut. Being imaginative can help us to see the solutions to problems and to overcome obstacles; it keeps our brains thinking flexibly. Imagination is also an easy blissful escape from reality – it's totally free fun, and there are no limits to it. Being imaginative is SO good for us!

But if you're out of practice, then you can sometimes be faced with that blank page fear when it comes to Being Imaginative. Imaginations need exercise just like bodies do. The thing about being imaginative is you don't have to start from scratch. Just a small development from something that already exists is your imagination at play.

An easy favourite to get you started is to ask yourself: what would I do if I won the lottery tomorrow? Filling in the details of what your day would look like as a millionaire inspires lots of little ideas that actually don't require money to achieve. Or another one I ask myself a lot is, if I owned that run-down building over there, what would I do with it?

Being playful takes some imagination. It's about seeing and seeking out the opportunities to bring more playfulness into your everyday. I've trained myself to look for those opportunities – those little moments of imagination that keep me entertained in my head and make the days all that more playful and enjoyable. Even dragging myself out for jog, I imagine I'm just doing the last 5k of a marathon and that there'll be applause and anything I want to eat at the end. (Or that I'm in training for a jungle survival experience.)

To get that imagination firing, I find it's best to either think big and fill in the details piece by piece to get you to the end goal, or start with a tiny inspiration and let it snowball . . .

Cascade in the details

- You've just been given a 'This is Your Life' book!
- Who's your dream celeb presenting it to you?
- What is the cover like?
- You open the cover. What are the four chapter headings?
- Wow! Each chapter has a song with lyrics adapted specifically to you. What are your life's jams?

Snowballing

So many things are best started with the end in mind. But in this activity, let's tear up that idea. Instead, think of yourself as a witness to where your mind is roaming. Look on with wonder at what is springing out of you.

5-minute imagination workouts

If you're still recovering from being told to stop gazing out the window when you were at school, getting used to flexing those imagination muscles again can take a bit of practice. But working your imagination is a brilliant life skill that you can get better at the more you do it. And the best part is, of course, you can do it ANYWHERE! Go on an adventure of thoughts with these quick HIIT exercises for your imagination.

Who are they?

When you're out and about – in a café, on the bus, waiting in a queue at the Post Office – look around you and spot someone you don't know. Then start to imagine a whole life for them – What's their name? Where are they from? What's their favourite song? What's their juicy secret? When did they last have sex? Who with? Who is their role model? What really winds them up? What's their most treasured possession? What was the last book they read? When was the last time they cried?

The meet cute

Up the ante: pick two people – maybe one of them is the same person as above – and make them meet in your mind. How do they know each other? What happens next? Now turn this into an Oscar-nominated film of next year. What genre is it? Maybe a horror?! Place them in peril – will one save the other or just save themselves and get the hell out of there? With every decision, take the story on another unexpected twist full of suspense and intrigue.

3D doodling

A scrap of paper can be torn into a mountain range or folded into a tiny concertina fan. The metal cage from the top of a prosecco bottle can be reworked into a tortoise or a chair. A small family of mini-mice can materialise from some bits of Blu Tack on your desk. Like doodling with a pen or pencil (see page 24), reimagining everyday items and shaping them to your will can activate different parts of your brain, help you focus and encourage divergent thinking – the scientific way of describing the generation of lots of bright ideas. (See also page 50 for more on unusual uses of everyday objects.)

Jail birds

Amy, general manager of Drink, Shop & Do, came up with this idea: if you interact with a lot of different people at work, pretend you're all in prison together and decide what crimes they have committed. From petty theft to serial murder . . . you'll never look at your boss the same way again.

What if?

A classic but a goodie: what would you spend your lottery win on? Or, if you were Mayor/King/ Queen for the day, what would you do? What if you had an extra hour every day . . . how would you make use of it? What is your superpower and how would you use it – where do you stand in the battle of good vs evil?

Interiors

When you're in a new space, look around and get all *Changing Rooms*. How would you redesign the space? Would you rip out those windows? Install a home bar? What colour would you paint the ceiling? Really think about how the room is laid out and set up – how the space flows and defined areas lead into others. This is a great way to work out spacial awareness skills too.

Role play

Not everyone's cup of tea, but pretending you're someone else can improve empathy and social interaction skills – plus it's just fun to try out a different life for a while. 'Meet' a friend for the first time and find out about each other's lives. *You used to roadie for Annie Mac?* How int-er-rest-ing . . .

A drawing of two halves

Cut out a picture from a magazine or newspaper – it could be a face, a landscape, the interior of a room . . . Fold it in half and place it on a piece of blank paper. Now draw the missing half – but let your imagination lead. Maybe there are UFOs landing in your living room or Cara Delevingne has an extra couple of beautiful eyes . . .

INK SPLATS

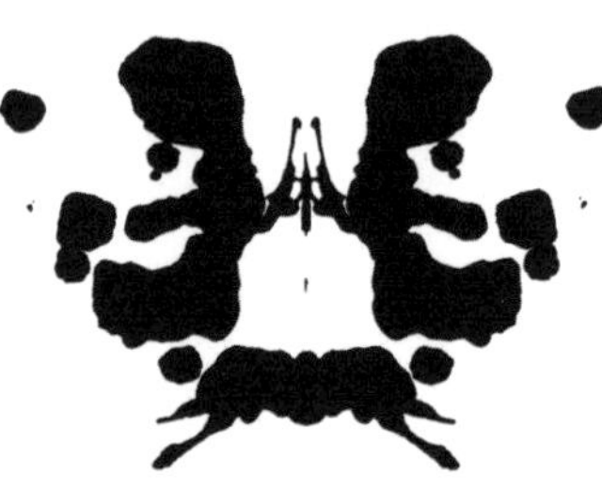

What do you see? Based on the famous Rorschach test, what do these symmetrical ink blots mean to you? Do you see a fluffy bunny hopping out of a hat, or a demon from the deep coming straight for you? Embellish them with your own illustrations . . .

INK SPLATS

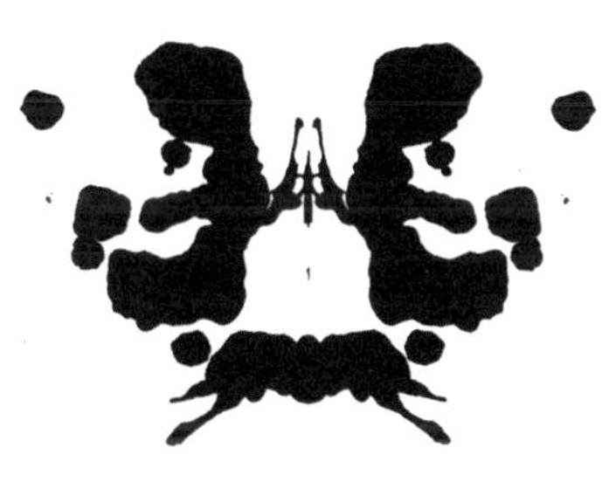

What do you see? Based on the famous Rorschach test, what do these symmetrical ink blots mean to you? Do you see a fluffy bunny hopping out of a hat, or a demon from the deep coming straight for you? Embellish them with your own illustrations . . .

Imagining your future – dream big!

The Law of Attraction works by focusing positively on a specific goal until it manifests in your life. Some people see it as the unquestionable magic of the universe answering your call – you appeal to the universe in all its infinite unknowable mysteries, and, lo, it shall provide!

Although many people really believe in the Power of the Universe, a more earthly interpretation is that once you have a freshly imagined endgame in mind for yourself, you will inevitably adjust how you navigate and view the world, introducing subtle changes to your day-to-day, making the effort to reach out and talk to different people, attracting positive energy by giving out positivity, and bit by bit shaping your existence until you have realised your vision. It's a bit like the less scientific idea of 'fake it till you make it', except that there is some impressive anecdotal research to back it up. Imagine yourself doing something and if you think it hard enough, it will happen!

This is actually a proven technique some elite athletes use to enhance performance in competitions. Imagining a movement has been shown to activate the associated movement areas in the brain, so you prepare for the action – basically giving your brain a practice run before you do the real-life run. In a similar way, writing your goals down first – or putting them on a vision board or however you want to set them in place – and then imagining how you might reach them will start your brain thinking about how to achieve them. You may not know *consciously* how to achieve them yet, but it is thought that your brain will be working behind the scenes, mapping out some possible routes. As Harvard professor Srini Pillay says: 'Imagining activates brain regions that can unconsciously map your path to success.'

How we approach life can have a huge impact on the world around us and on

ourselves. Giving out positive energy, focusing on the good, prioritising good moods, keeping striving forwards, and booting out the Negative Nellies and Debbie Downers in our circles, means we will attract all that glowing energy back to ourselves. We are mirrors – so what we give out we will see coming back to us.

You can use the Law of Attraction for anything you want the universe to help you with – luring money, gaining a #strong bod and/or finding love are three of the most popular, but it can be anything. A broke Jim Carrey wrote himself a cheque for a 10 million dollars dated ten years in the future that he kept in his wallet. A decade passed and he landed a role on *Dumb and Dumber* . . . It worked for him, so dream big!

Test the Law of Attraction – in a low-key way

Here's another idea from Amy (general manager at Drink, Shop & Do). Pick a random object that you want to attract and manifest in your life – don't tell anyone what it is as this might jinx your chance of seeing it organically. It has to be something you wouldn't see in a normal day, e.g. a stripy orange ball or a saxophone. Now you leave it to the universe. Usually, you'll just forget about it, but then when you see it – which could be weeks or months later – it's a really exciting event because it's so random! The pure joy when you spot your item is GREAT! Give it a go!

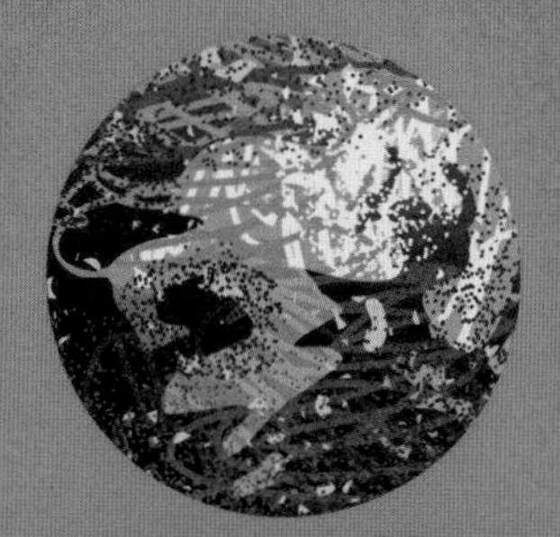

Introducing future you

Close your eyes and imagine you are five, ten, fifteen years in the future. You're at a HILARIOUS dinner party and have met a FABULOUS person who is sitting next to you and topping up your glass with premium champagne. Tell them who you are and what your life is like. Really let your imagination run away with you . . .

Questions your dining companion might ask you. Write your answers underneath . . .

1. What do you do for work? What do you most love about it?

....

2. Your home sounds WONDERFUL – tell me about it!

....

3. What are your proudest accomplishments?

....

4. What are you doing next weekend?

....

5. What do you like most about our host tonight?

....

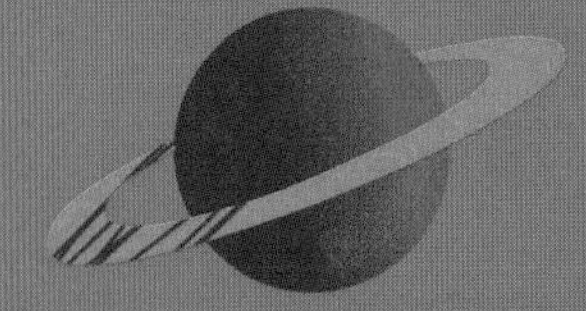

After you're done, pick out the key aspects that made you feel excited about your dream life. Think about how you can introduce some of these into your life now so you can actually become that person you imagined you could be. You may need to tone some of these expectations a bit – or not! – it's not really about the specifics as much as the 'feel' of your imagined future yourself.

Take it one step further and make yourself a vision board: cut out pictures from magazines and stick those key aspects of your future self's existence to a piece of card, paper or inside the pages of a notebook – and also see the exercises on page 67 about celebrating your own unique version of creativity. Look at it often, really imagine what it WILL be like when you achieve and realise all these amazing aspects of the brilliant future You 2.0.

'Imagination is the beginning of creation. You imagine what you desire, you will what you imagine and at last you create what you will.' George Bernard Shaw

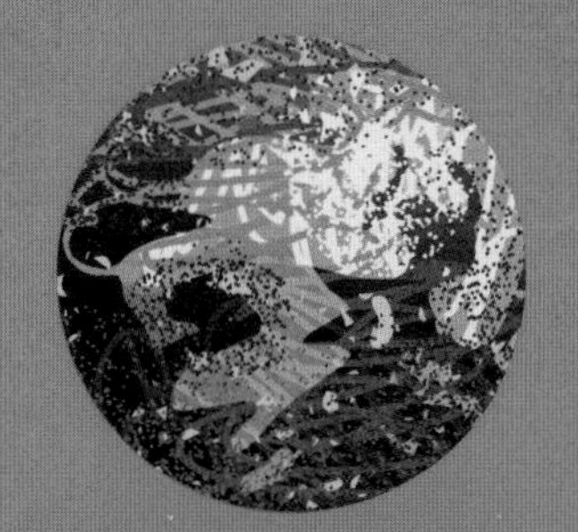

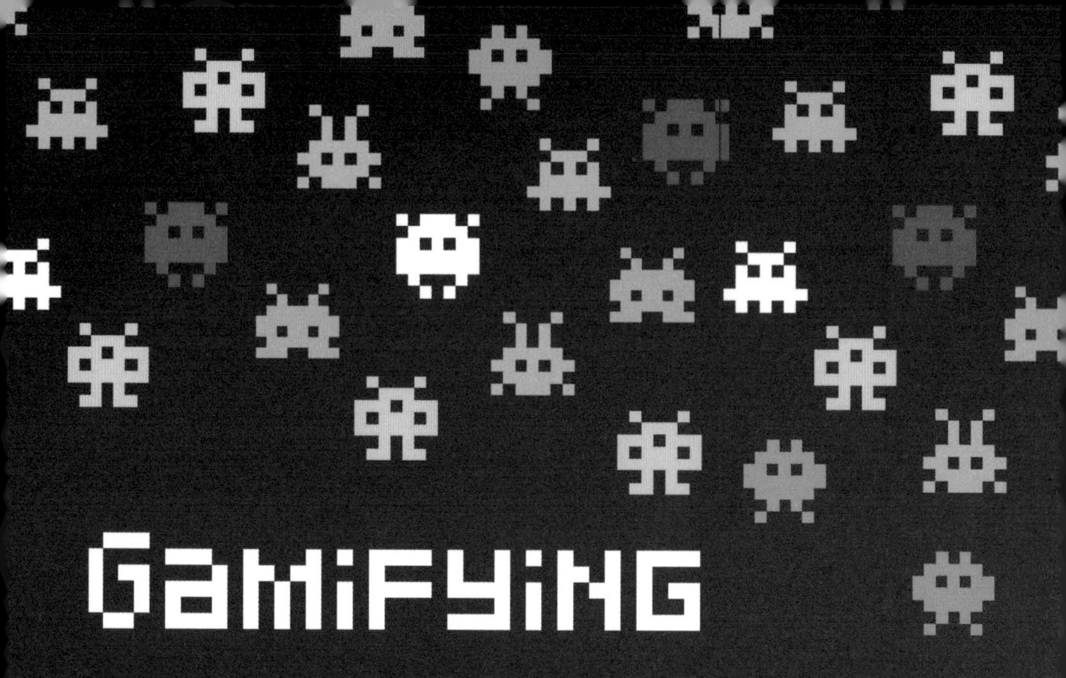

Gamifying

We all need to take the bins out and go to work. These are the unavoidable tasks of being a functioning human adult. But rather than see them as gross chores on an endless to-do list, let's reframe them and turn them into games.

Gamifying is the act of making everyday tasks more fun. From keeping track of how many steps we walk each day, how many hours we sleep and how many glasses of water we drink on our phones or watches, to those colourful, all-pinging, all-dancing apps for everything from banking and investing in the stock market, to meditation and yoga, gamification appeals to our human nature by encouraging progress and reward, in the form of scores, achievement levels and bonus points. Even if we don't get a physical reward to hold in our hands, we still feel that glowing sense of achievement once we complete a task – or when we have successfully evaded the living dead on a Zombies, Run!

Bringing elements of gameplay into our day-to-day gives our minds a challenge to work on, with satisfying 'wins' that give us little dopamine and serotonin hits, the pleasure and reward circuits in our brains, and we love it. (See more about our friend dopamine on page 18.) Reframing tasks as FUN also reduces cortisol – our stress hormone – as we are encouraged to complete potentially overwhelming, taxing or just plain dull activities in a more playful way. Gamification also looks to break down tasks into smaller, more manageable steps, allowing our brain to really focus in on one element at a time, encouraging better attention and improved learning and recall.

Hunter-gatherer societies tend to involve a lot of play in their daily lives and work, and are known to be pretty laid-back, relaxed societies. The importance they place on play and fun, both as children and adults, reduces aggression and encourages cooperation. And, despite their seeming lack of security, they tend to cope with stress far better than the majority of us in the more 'developed' world. So, let's be more hunter-gatherer as we tackle our to-do lists. We can reframe anything to become a game: you can play a game in your head so no one even needs to know, or make it big part of your team's approach at work. Adding a layer of ridiculousness makes life more light-hearted and the day swing by more enjoyably.

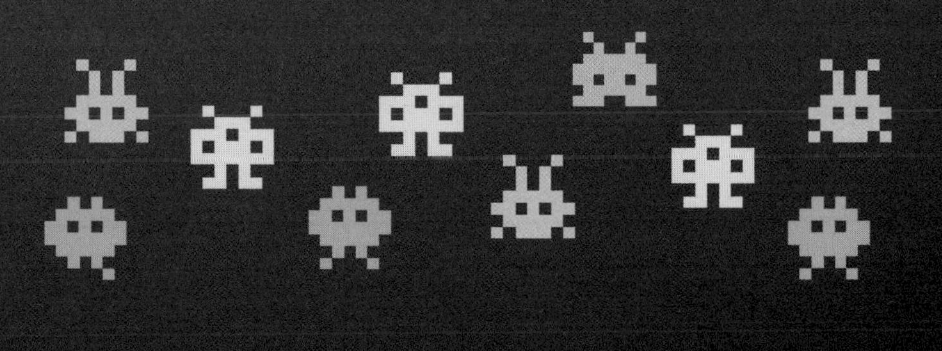

How to Gamify Anything

Games need rules and wins. When you have arduous tasks or a daunting goal ahead of you, find something within it that you could give yourself points for. If you are currently looking at a really boring, long or difficult to-do list, this can sometimes feel an impossible feat in itself, but there will be something! It could be as simple as that little feel-good hit from beating your personal best (quickest bathroom clean ever!) or even just the satisfaction of completing each stage of a complicated work assignment.

You need to celebrate your successes! This is the important bit. Link a small physical gesture to it, like High Fives all round or fist bumps or your ultimate power poses – take a photo! Or plan something nice to do at the end of each task – bribery works a treat – but glory is usually the best incentive.

5-minute tricks to gamify your day and make even boring chores FUN!

1

Break jobs into stages; as you move on to each part, change outfits, write in a new ink colour, listen to a new album, or move to a different location – preferably a café with a new cake selection.

2

Trying to give up sugar? Want to exercise before work? Aiming to be creative every day? We all love a star chart – and a coffee shop loyalty card! So make yourself a life loyalty card. Ten gold stars = two episodes of the show you're trying not to binge-watch.

3

When on the phone with tedious people, echo the Euro 96 England football team – answer with song lyrics.

4

Eat your way through a rainbow of fruit and veg, ticking off colours as you go. Don't underestimate the power of treats.

5

On your boring weekly grocery shop, pick up a new ingredient or fun item from each aisle to complement the rice, washing-up liquid and kitchen foil essentials.

Imaginative flow

As we know, one of the main rules of flow is you need to feel as though you're achieving something (see page 37). You need to experience a sense of progression, overcoming challenges and moving up. Sometimes exercising our imaginations can feel a bit passive – allowing our brains to wander freely and throw us unexpected ideas – a brain doodle, if you like. There's often not really that sense of dedicated focus or any real aim.

This has some great benefits, of course: free-flowing thought can result in links between ideas we would never have considered, which is at the core of innovative thinking. And it can be a great way to give our brains a 'rest' from everyday taskmaster jobs. But imaginative flow exercises allow us to train our brains to focus on imaginative tasks, helping strengthen those skills, so we can call on them more readily when we need to. Also, a state of flow is an enjoyable place for our brains to be, so we should try to get it there as often as we can.

Reading – whatever material you're reading (no judgement) this is one of the quickest ways to reach a state of flow. Have you ever nearly missed your stop because you're too engrossed in the complex lives of those characters on the page? Reading ignites the imagination and allows you to get lost in other worlds. See page 134 for more on the power of books.

Writing – like reading, conjuring imaginary worlds and people onto the page is a fast-track way to get into a flow state. The story goes that Kerouac wrote *On the Road* in three weeks on a continuous roll of paper, so as not to break his flow. Whether true or not, or whether drugs were involved or not, is up for debate . . .

Nail polish marbling

You will need:

- Paper or objects to marble, like a jam jar
- Nail polishes: at least two colours, but as many as you want! Old ones work fine
- Masking tape
- Stirring stick (a wooden kebab skewer or toothpick)
- Plastic tub: bigger than the object you're marbling, preferably one you're throwing away
- Gloves or Vaseline to protect your fingers

Instructions

1

Cover with tape any areas of you'd like to remain free of nail polish. This is especially good for adding a clean straight line.

2

Fill a plastic tub with water, then pour in nail polish – dot it around the water's surface and swirl it with the stirring stick. Two or three colours are recommended.

3

Gently lower the surface you'd like to marble onto the floating polish.

4

Immediately and carefully lift it away – the pattern will come with it!

5

Set aside to dry for 15 minutes, then pat the water droplets with a paper towel. Remove the tape and voilà ! It's that easy.

6

Use the stirring stick to collect the rest of the nail polish and to clean up the water for the next dip.

Breathing space to imagine

Sometimes, when you've got lots on or you're just feeling the pressure of *LIFE* (gah!), it can feel as if the ability to be imaginative and playful has completely left you. Poof! Out the window. But these are exactly the times when you need to find a way to be MORE playful. Life is for exploring, experimenting and having fun. It will have its ups and downs, of course, but it's so important to try to still see the world around you with a little wonder and magic, even during the tough days – and not just as a whole pile of stress.

To set your mind at ease and make room inside for a little playfulness, we need to free up some headspace for your imagination to roam. Your wilder ideas need space to grow: they can't be cooped up inside a busy head.

Being told to simply 'clear your mind', though, is an almost impossible and very unhelpful instruction. The mind needs stuff to work on, otherwise you'll spiral. So you need to replace whatever is preoccupying your mind with some fresh topics.

It can be helpful to visualise our mind as brainwaves. Sometimes they are moving fast because there's so much to do and we're anxious about it. When we're in this state, picture the waves as very tight – a high frequency, if you like. Let's try to loosen them up . . . One way you can shift your brainwaves into a nice open, steady, bouncy frequency – perfect for letting in a little imagination and creativity – is to fill your mind with something that has a nice, steady rhythm to match.

Our lungs just happen to be the perfect size – a deep inhale and exhale provide a great length of wave to focus on.

- Start by counting the breath in – maybe to four or five counts.
- Then count it out to the same amount.
- After five breaths, increase the count by one, and keep doing this until you can feel the breath stretching the lungs wide and your belly contracting to fully empty your lungs on the exhale. Imagine your brainwaves rising and falling as you inhale and exhale in nice, calm, slow arcs.

When your mind is on overdrive, you might need to add another layer of difficulty, until you feel that the exercise is taking your full attention (almost a flow activity!). You can add a further visualisation – maybe you can imagine your breath as being circular and as you exhale, you're squeezing it up your spine, like pushing toothpaste through a tube, and as you inhale it's softly trickling down the front of your body like a waterfall, filling up the bowl of your belly.

Or, if you're not as into your visual thinking, you can make the counting of your breath more complicated by adding breath holds.

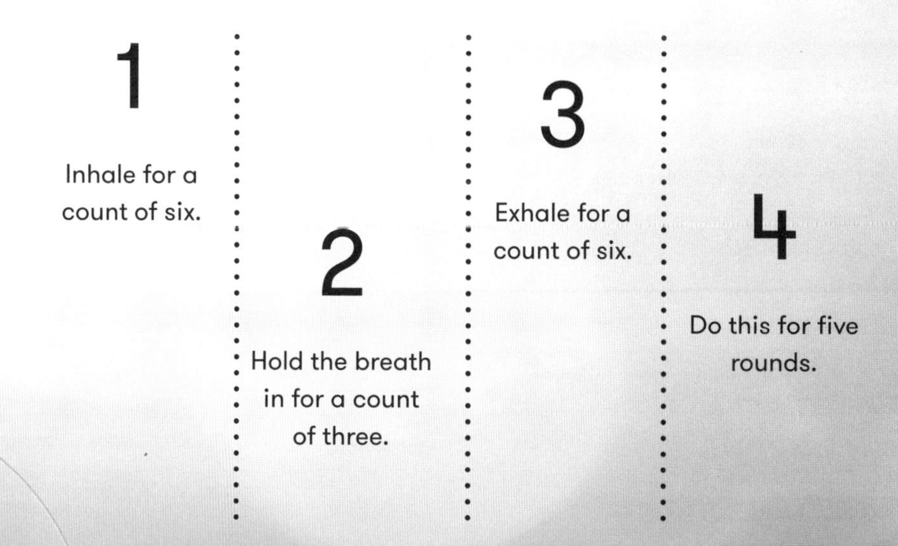

If, at first, counting the rounds is hard, use your fingers to help you remember. Then switch to holding on empty. You can start to get really creative with these exercises. How many rounds can you do before your mind loses track of the count? Keep a note of your PB and try to beat yourself next time. How long can you stretch your breath? (Don't play this one for too long or you'll get light-headed!) How complicated can you make the in-hold-out-hold pattern and still remember it? In for six, hold for two, out for six, hold for four – just always make the exhale equal or longer than the in-breath.

Another great way to help calm your breathing or make a more complicated breath pattern is to close one nostril at a time with your finger. This kind of breathing is popular in yoga and is thought to bring increased energy and focus into your body.

1	2	3	4	5
Rest the first two fingers of your right hand between your eyebrows. Hover thumb and ring finger either side of your nose.	Press your thumb down and breathe in through your left side.	Press your ring finger down and lift your thumb, then exhale through the right side.	Breathe in through the thumb (right) side again.	Switch fingers, exhale through the left nostril. Repeat five times.

Once you've calmed your mind through rhythmic breath work, you'll find yourself more open to ideas and less weighed down. Let your imagination flourish – try the activity on the next page, with no limits!

Melody Travers (melodytravers.net) has started a drawing of a mythical creature. Finish it as wildly as you can imagine. Maybe they have 2 heads or 7 legs or a long snout?

Reading is the easiest way to activate our imaginations

Every day we are exposed to more incoming information than at any other point in our history. Our ancestors would have been terrified by the amount of new knowledge, ideas and waste-of-time mind junk we force our brains to process and filter over a 24-hour period. In many ways, this is an amazing leap forwards for humanity – infinite shared wisdom and endless ways to be inspired. (You can read more about this on page 210.)

But how many of us actually sit down and quietly read a book these days? A depressing study in the US reported that 42 per cent of college graduates don't read a single book after graduation. And there are plenty of other surveys that suggest that reading, in general and across all age groups and social sectors, is definitely on the decline. With so much good TV available, this is not really a shocker to any of us. But we need to get back into reading more books!

First there are all the obvious benefits of regular reading: we learn things and it helps keep our brains active. We also know that our attention span these days is pretty embarrassing, as we find ourselves flicking from screen to screen and task to task; reading a book, without the distractions of flashing ads down the side of the page, is a great way to improve your ability to focus on one job at a time.

Then there are the psychological and emotional benefits. To become fully immersed in a book, to conjure up detailed imagery of a made-up world, to hold the emotional inner lives of characters together as you progress through the plot, anticipating their moves and actions, requires you to block out everything else. Getting properly involved in a book lands you square in a flow state, which we know our brain loves (see page 12). It quietens down the noise of your own emotional inner life while you pay attention to the turmoil of your new fictional friends. Getting into a state of flow can

'Fiction can show you a different world. It can take you somewhere you've never been. Once you've visited other worlds, like those who ate fairy fruit, you can never be entirely content with the world that you grew up in. Discontent is a good thing: discontented people can modify and improve their worlds, leave them better, leave them different.' Neil Gaiman

help ease anxiety, slowing down our breathing and whirring brains, and if you read before bed, it can help you drift off to sleep. Reading can also help your writing skills and improves your vocabulary. And if it's a complicated plot then you are giving your brain a real workout, stretching those cognitive and analytic skills. Which, in turn, leaves you better able to problem-solve in the real world.

Being able to imagine the other side of an obstacle or challenge – through the dilemmas that the characters we read about are facing – helps us to feel more empowered in our own decision-making, too. Maybe we agree with their motivations, or maybe we're screaming at them: WHY?! Either way, we gain confidence in our ability to trust our own instincts. Being able to imagine a different set of circumstances can also help us to shape the life we truly want. It gives us some control over our existence, meaning we feel better equipped to deal with events that may occur outside of what we can control. Building up our self-assurance and confidence helps our nervous system stay calm in the face of life's challenges.

Your choice of reading material can make a difference, too. If the story you're reading bears similarities to what's going on in your own life or includes characters you connect with on a personal level, their actions and responses can help you process feelings and emotions you may be experiencing yourself. This is especially helpful if you're not all that great at acknowledging your feelings. Evidence shows that readers tend to process their own emotions better because they learn about them through the characters they read about, and as a consequence they understand themselves better too.

Conversely, if you're reading about the plights and

experiences of people who are very different from you, then this can help develop empathy and understanding, leading to more tolerance and less division. Reading can help create a utopian society!

Perhaps most importantly, though, reading is maybe the quickest way to activate our imagination. Within a sentence or two, you're transported somewhere else. It gives your brain a much-needed escape. You can hang out with anyone, do anything, literally anywhere – you can even time travel! It's fun and encourages us to think about possibilities other than those we are used to. Reading fiction stretches our imaginations, opening us up to novel ideas (ha!). It allows us to see through the eyes of other people and live their lives.

A quick sidebar on sci-fi: China has a long history of being pretty scathing of science-fiction, even going so far as to consider it a harmful influence on its people. But in recent years it's hit the big time. At a 2007 science-fiction and fantasy convention in China – believed to be the first Party-approved one to take place – Neil Gaiman asked why the change of heart. He was told that the Chinese had been good at making things, but not at innovating. They couldn't 'imagine'. So they went to the US and visited Apple, Microsoft and Google – all the companies shaping our global futures. They discovered that their employees had all read science-fiction as children. Sci-fi has since been booming in China – some even saying it is its biggest export since kung-fu – and alongside it, innovation and invention has bloomed.

So let's get back to fiction. Let's read before bed, on the bus, instead of bingeing on TV. Let's listen to audiobooks, read out loud to each other, join libraries, start book clubs and work our way through that towering to-be-read pile. Our minds, imaginations and entire selves will benefit – and maybe you'll even dream up the future of technology from between those pages.

EXPERT IN PLAY

HASTE THEATRE COMPANY

Haste is a unified force of five women who create fantastical worlds to portray the everyday. We are multilingual actors, clowns, dancers, creators, puppeteers, singers and friends. Fusing comedy and tragedy, the ugly and the beautiful, we shock, stimulate and entertain. We create magic through simplicity and haunting harmonies. Our playfulness and energy is infectious.

As performers, when we are in a playful state, we have a heightened awareness of the present moment. We feel a childlike innocence. We are not distracted by inhibitions and judgments. Over seven years of working together we have developed deeper relationships and an intangible connection through playing games and being playful together. It almost goes without saying that being playful lifts the spirits – making fertile ground for creative work.

Playfulness as an adult is vital to living a life that isn't too heavy and complex. If we are able to play from time to time and unleash that childlike quality within ourselves, the body feels lighter, more alive and things tend to flow more easily. From a psychological point of view, play is seen by writers such as D. W. Winnicott as a crucial part of life. In his book *Playing and Reality*, he states:

'It is in playing and only in playing that the individual child or adult is able to be creative and to use the whole personality, and it is only in being creative that the individual discovers the self.'

When devising shows Haste Theatre use play as a means to create work. Through playing, we are able to tap into our imaginations and enter another state of being, where we work with each other on a different level. We play to find unexpected ideas or ways into a character or scene creation. Many physical theatre companies use play to warm up the body and mind to be free and receptive. Play should be celebrated and respected as a means to finding a common goal and motivation, and seeing the journey and experience of the game itself as a way to create material.

Fast, dirty, bad

The aim of this exercise is to create freely without expectation or hesitation. It is similar to free writing, except it starts from a stimulus in the form of a short character profile (see below), best given to you by someone else. You read the profile, then you sit and write for 20 minutes without stopping and just see what comes out. The title gives you the freedom to do it quickly and without feeling like it needs to be good. You will most likely be pleasantly surprised with this exercise. It's easily achievable. with a great outcome, no matter what the content at the end. You could even try monologuing them to the mirror if writing's not your thing.

- Richard, 50, ex-alcoholic bachelor, has turned his hand to ballroom dancing in order to find a partner.
- Sarah, teacher, loves rollerblading on the weekends and would rather be a diamond dealer than shout at snotty kids all day.
- Harry, 35, lives with his parents, wildly frustrated, very pompous and proud, plays golf competitively.
- Sadia, 22 just graduated Cambridge and finds herself in a complicated love triangle that is throwing her off her job interview preparation.
- Ashley's cat video just went viral for the all wrong reasons. She can't bear the spotlight and wants the attention to disappear but every response is making it worse.

WELCOME to your IMAGINARIUM

Remember all those pretend worlds you created when you were a kid? Fantasy lands on distant planets, sailing boats made from boxes, sheets strung up into tents in the Sahara in your back garden?

All those made-up places, people, animals and extreme modes of transport enriched your creativity and made you happy. Children don't tend to focus as much on the reality of their worlds as adults do – why would they? Is there anything more B.O.R.I.N.G. than the real world? As we get older, our imagination tends to be dragged down

by the most yawn-worthy killjoy of all: logic. And with it, we learn to navigate the world like adult humans. OK, so that's pretty essential – but not ALL the time. We already know we love a bit of escapism through watching films, reading books, or some good old-fashioned daydreaming (see page 162). And we know that it is good for us, too.

Imagination is focused on creating something out of nothing. It takes the tiny beginnings of an idea and leads you . . . who knows where! Literally wherever you want.

Every choice you make in all aspects of your life starts with using your imagination as you consider where this plan you have in mind might take you. You ask yourself: what will this experience be like? Will I enjoy it? Flexing and developing your imagination is vital to learning how to listen to your inner self so you can make better choices for *you*. Optimistic people tend to have better imaginations and practise using them more often – they can literally imagine a brighter world for themselves (see also the Law of Attraction on page 120). And a healthy obsession with sci-fi can lead to imagining technologies of the future (see page 137).

So let's ditch dull old logic for a bit, think beyond the rules and expectations of your normal every day and take a trip through the deeper recesses of your imaginarium . . . Who knows what's lurking in there?! Let's find out . . .

A date with your imagination

LET'S START WITH AN EASY ONE:

- Imagine you're sitting on a chair at a table. Where are you? Make it somewhere you've never been before. What kind of chair and table is it? What can you see in front of you? What's your view? Are you on holiday? Are you even on Earth?
- How do you feel? What mood are you in? Feel those emotions fully as though you were really there.
- There's a meal in front of you on the table. What is it? What does it look like? Smell like? Take a bite – what does it taste like? Really imagine those senses – these will be partly based on reality and your experience of other meals you've eaten, but expand on those. Keep adding layers to your experience. Use all your senses.
- Who is with you? Who else lives in this fantasy land of yours? What do they look like? How do they get around? How do they communicate? Are you, in fact, telepathic? Do the animals rule you? Do you live underground?

Now – Boom! Let's change a fundamental law of physics . . . just for the fun of it:

- o Maybe there's no gravity – what happens next? Where does your dinner go? How do people move around?
- o Maybe there's no day or night. Or maybe we are all nocturnal and sleep in the day – what does this mean for how we go about our lives?
- o What's that?! Is that time looping round again?

Let the world you find yourself in be governed by a whole new set of rules. Question the accepted limitations you're so used to living within and upturn those accepted parameters you usually follow so obediently. Challenging what we are used to and what we see as the norm helps us see things from a totally different perspective and explore new angles. Maybe some of the rules you've always lived by don't appeal to you anymore? See what you can bring back from your made-up world to take with you as you next head out the door . . .

EXPERT IN PLAY

THE ROBIN COLLECTIVE
THEROBINCOLLECTIVE.CO.UK
HOUSE OF TOAST

We love toasters. Not only are they great for a quick snack, they can also be a clever – and unexpected – creative tool.

We started our toasty architectural endeavours numerous years back, whilst thinking up new cookery workshops. Yes, House of Toast is not exactly a fancy cookery course, but it is simple and huge fun for groups of friends at all levels of imagination.

Each team or competitor must have a standard two-slice toaster, which they are welcome to theme as needed with their team name and creations. We've had everything from 'Buffy the Crumb Slayer' to 'Pita Pan'. We normally have an hour for building (give or take) but spend a few minutes before each session going over the basics and mixing up some cocktails.

There are seven golden rules for House of Toast

1

No double toasting.
This includes putting additional slices into the toaster slots, but also putting slices on top of the toaster to save toasting time. We don't like fire hazards.

2

Be kind. We love a good competition but we don't like rude people. Kindness brings rewards when we play.

3

Dance and be wild.
Make sure you put on good tunes throughout the game, just like our own DJ Baguetta would. Some of our favourites include 'Pump Up the Jam' by Technotronic and 'Breadfan' by Metallica.
How fitting!

4

Structures need to be fully standing throughout judging.
If it falls, you've failed.

5

You don't have to build a house. The more creative and narrative you get with your build, the better. We've seen a lot of London Bridges and we know you can think of something more clever.

6

No bread. This competition isn't called House of Bread. No. Toast! Builds must be entirely toasted unless it somehow (and we very rarely let it slide) fits into the narrative you've created.

7

One toaster per team.
Teams are only allowed ONE two-slice toaster, and for safety we ask that only one team member operates it.

To help keep the structures fixed, each team can also have a pot of toothpicks. We don't allow knives at the bar for obvious reasons, but we do encourage using items from team member's bags to be used as tools (i.e. keys or credit cards for cutting).

Finished pieces are great for smashing up and if you think your creation is worthy (like our Toast Mihal), leave it in a random, public place for a laugh.

4

THINK

The most frequent remark on my school reports was 'Coralie would do well if only she would stop looking out the window and daydreaming'. But I stand by this 'time-wasting' activity wholeheartedly. I believe it was spending so much time living in my little imagined dream world that led me to not only come up with the idea of Drink, Shop & Do but actually enabled me to fill in the details of how it would all work and come together. Dreaming and imagining is preparation for planning.

Getting lost in your own thoughts often leads to new ideas and new ways of doing things. I like to think of them as bubbles floating up to the conscious surface of my mind. If we get stuck doing things the same way we always have, thinking as we have done for years, we'll never get to experience anything different – anything that could potentially be better! It's new ideas and approaching problems from unexpected directions that keeps us feeling curious and playful.

Being playful is about attitude. It's about how we take on life – and whatever it throws our way. It's about how we think about and process everything around us. We can all be playful when we're playing a game, or be creative when we're sitting down and making something. But a playful attitude to life, whatever the circumstances, is the ultimate aim. Being open to new ideas and experiences makes you more adaptable and flexible, more able to go with a flow and less likely to lose your shit when things take an unexpected turn.

We naturally live with chatter going on in the background of our minds. Sometimes it's focused on stimuli from the world around us; sometimes it's wandering and incessant. Then at other times we get those precious moments of deep insightful clarity. But how much control do we really have over our thoughts? (And is the real us the 'we' or the 'thoughts'? I think my mind will implode if I carry on with this train of thought.) Don't think of a pink elephant. Hmm. We're certainly not the master of them, are we?

You can learn to think more quickly, look for connections between ideas and challenge the way you usually solve problems and approach life every day. You can discover your very own, unique way of thinking and being – that's wholly and entirely you and no one else. And that's definitely to be celebrated.

'You can discover more about a person in an hour of play than in a year of conversation'
– Plato

Mundane routines and the multiverse

There are theories abounding today – even by top-dog physicists – that there are potentially infinite universes, where each time we make a decision, however small, a new universe shoots off into existence with consequences that reach beyond that further and further into unknown paths.

Imagine yourself as the main character in one of those addictive, choose-your-own-ending books you read as a kid. Do you press the red button or the blue button? Turn to page 17 and you'll be either King of the Goblins or freefalling through space . . .

Something as simple as whether you get the 8.01 train or the 8.11 can *potentially* impact your world beyond your wildest dreams. The 8.01 could get you straight to work, no issues, same as usual. Getting the 8.11, however, might be where you trip up the stairs and are helped up by a mysterious, good-looking stranger where hearts explode around you and birds sing you both to the altar. Or . . . it could be that the train breaks down, meaning you miss your presentation, get fired and have to move back in with your parents. Deciding between a fancy-looking pastry to go with your coffee – or not – could lead to a conversation with your colleague about said pastry. That conversation might bring significant joy to your life and you might even learn that your colleague wants to set up a bakery – so do you! Ten years later you're hosting *Bake Off*. Or, your colleague might be so obsessed with your pastry, she forgets to tell you your boss wants to see you at 9.30am. You're a no-show, while she glares at you through the glass of her office door as you shove a cream puff in your face.

Whatever the outcome of each individual choice we make – multiverses or not – following the same routines can lead to stagnancy in all areas of our life. It's the exact opposite of living a playful, engaged existence. Before too long, we can find ourselves drifting through on autopilot. There's the old saying that 'madness is doing the same things over again and expecting different results'. Well, this kind of applies to life in general. Don't sleep through life: wake up and smell something different from your usual flat white. Be flexible, be open to change and new ideas. It will make you more adaptable and more fun to be around. Keep everyone – including yourself – on their toes.

In this potential multiverse, make every day an adventure. If you're not sure how to shake things up, start with the basics. Even the smallest changes can have a big impact.

To get you started on your road to innovation, take a look at your daily routine. Yes, you've probably carefully honed it since high school, but turn it upside down and see what happens. You might just see the world in different ways, find yourself interacting with new people, have excitingly refreshing conversations and think bigger, more dynamic thoughts. And from there, who knows where you'll end up!

Quick ways to break up your routine and change your thinking

In the left-hand column of your notebook, write out your regular activities, including details of times, what you usually eat, wear, routes you tread, etc. And then in the opposite column, write a totally different alternative. If you're not sure where to start, pretend you're someone else, do what you think they'd do and fake it till you make it.

For example

- Get up at 7am every morning? Get up at 5.30am and watch the sun rise.
- Always have toast and coffee? Have a hot chocolate and a bacon roll.
- Jeans and a T-shirt? Business suits today!

- Everyday trudge to the station? Find another route that excites you.
- Lunchtime at your desk? NO! Go to a gallery, meet a friend, meditate or read a book.
- Slump on the sofa and watch TV when you get home? Ban the TV for a week.
- You don't have to eat dinner food at dinner time. Have a picnic or eat breakfast in the evening.
- Sleep with your head up at the headboard? Try sleeping the other way, with your head where your feet usually go.
- Tend to read or look at the same people's work for inspiration? Try someone new – maybe someone you don't even like!
- Think you do most of your best work in the afternoon? Try getting up at dawn, or staying awake until 3am.

Clear your mind

Do thirty minutes of continuous writing – preferably when you first get up. Don't think about it – put down anything you like, you don't even need to be able to read your own handwriting, just let a stream of consciousness flow without stopping. Once the chatter of your mind is on paper you can leave it there and make space for new thoughts.

Clear your doubts

How would you approach this next thing you're doing if you knew there was no chance of anything negative happening? You've already won. You didn't make a fool of yourself. Everyone loves your idea. You're a natural.

Flip to your creative spacial brain

Drawing Pyrolettes (Face Profile Vases) is one of the best ways to relax, concentrate and change the mode of your brain. Imagine drawing a human face profile, left or right. Then on the opposite side, draw the mirror effect of the same profile. Fill an A4 sheet with 20 pyrolettes. Get faster!

Learning through play

Play is one of the very best ways to learn a new skill. Do you remember anything other than how bored you were from those lessons where your teacher made you copy down pages and pages of notes from an ever-rolling blackboard?

But everyone remembers the fun classes when you took your work outside or dressed up and re-enacted Robin Hood. In fact, play has been recognised as so vital to children's development that the right to play was named a basic human need by the UN Convention on the Rights of the Child.

Breaktime goes beyond simply creating mayhem in the playground, though, teaching us many essential skills needed for life. From navigating those complex classroom relationships to how to cook a roast dinner in your play kitchen at home, and the etiquette of manners that must be displayed at a tea party (whether your guests are teddy bears or not). Playtime also bonds us together as we learn empathy, helping

‘The creation of something new is not accomplished by the intellect, but by the play instinct.’
Carl Jung

us work out who we can trust and who’s best avoided. Reduced playtime in childhood has been linked to increased anxiety and depression – and some studies have even associated a lack of play with people who go on to commit murder.

It’s not much different when we hit adulthood. Play is so important to our continued development. But as adults, learning is usually a choice – compared with when we were at school – so in a way, because we are actively *choosing* to learn, we are able to return more easily to the happy, playful, carefree state of accidental learning of our childhood.

Depending on what you choose to learn, developing fresh skills can make you a more attractive employee too. Even if your new capabilities aren’t directly related to your job, mastering a tricky technique outside of the workplace can give you a new self-confidence in your abilities, which in turn can build others’ confidence in you. Learning also keeps life interesting and exciting, making us better at thinking on the spot and coming up with new ideas. As we know, the same-old-same-old breeds more of the old same-old (see page 152), so learning new things can give everything a fresh spark of energy and a brand-new perspective. Learning is also like taking your brain to the gym. It used to be thought that we didn’t have the capacity to produce new brain cells past adolescence, but this is old news! As adults we are perfectly able to develop new pathways in our brains and build new synapses, which help us think more quickly and in different ways. We are never too old to learn a fresh skill. Continual learning can boost your memory, power up that grey matter and help stave off an ageing brain.

There are other practical, in-the-world benefits too: life is changing around us quickly, and if we don’t keep up it can sometimes feel as though we might slip too far behind to catch up. We need to stay up to date, not only to feel relevant in the society in which we live, but so we can take advantage of all the amazing new opportunities that become open to us as a result. Once we get involved, whether that's through learning a new techy life skill or understanding what the latest trends are, the world won't seem so daunting and full of the unknown. Learning – particularly through play – also teaches us that it is perfectly OK to make mistakes, and that it is from our mistakes that we often learn the most. (See page 176 for more on the success of failure.)

But all this learned talk doesn't mean you now have to enrol at your local college on a Psychology 101 course, or attend a series of lectures on The Science of Space. Find something you want to learn that brings you joy and it won't even feel like school. There are millions of subjects, techniques and ideas to explore that will bring you all the benefits of newfound knowledge, and plenty of low-key ways to gain new skills (no notebook required), as well as some proven techniques to help you retain what you have learned.

How to win at learning

Multi-dimensional

Read it, listen to it, watch it, talk about it, dance it out if you like. If you want to fully understand something, learn about it in mixed media. Podcasts, online videos, books, talks, group seminars (feel free to interpret this quite loosely – a group of mates down the pub counts) or one-to-one tutorials. Even just chatting to interesting people who know more than you do. These are all ways to take in information and store it in different parts of your brain, meaning you're more likely to remember it later. Some studies even recommend changing location, smelling aromatherapy oils or playing particular music to help lock in your learning.

Take a nap

As if we need any excuse! Napping has been proven to help consolidate learning, moving memories into a deeper part of our brains where they are less likely to be forgotten. So, after watching that YouTube tutorial on modern calligraphy, get under the covers for forty winks.

How experienced are you?

When we play, we learn through the experience of actually doing the thing. It's learning through your *internal* understanding of something, rather than your *intellectual* understanding and is much more effective. In yoga, for example, we are more likely to remember how to perform a pose or sequence when we actually do it, rather than being told how to, reading about it or even watching it. So, in the words of Nike: Just Do It! And you'll be more likely to remember how to do it again. Have a go at some of the playful skills and projects in this book and learn something new.

Use it or lose it

This is particularly relevant when it comes to your brain. Have you ever looked back at essays you wrote at college or tried to help an eight-year-old with their primary school maths homework and wondered how on earth you understood it at the time? Your brain is very tidy, so if we don't practise our new skills our brain doesn't think we need them anymore and will throw them out with the rubbish.

Botanical drawing

Absorb yourself in concentration with this step-by-step botanical drawing project by Samantha Medlycott, botanical artist and calligrapher. Find her on Instagram for more inspiration @jot_on.

All you need is paper, a pencil, a rubber and some drawing pens (ideally one fine 0.05 and one heavier, 0.1).

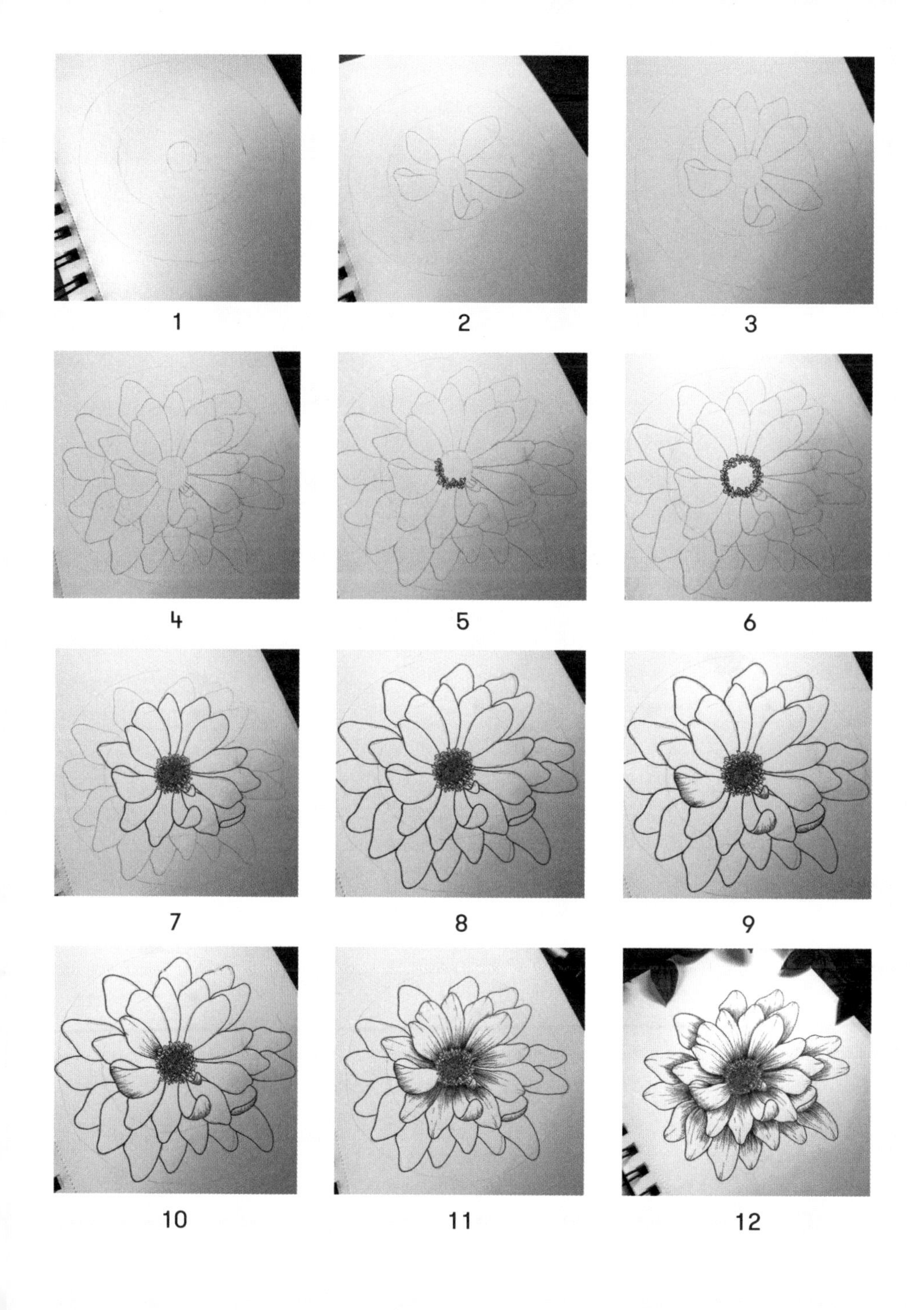
1
2
3
4
5
6
7
8
9
10
11
12

Make time for daydreaming

According to science, we spend almost 50 per cent of our days mentally clocked out of whatever activity we're supposed to be doing. That means nearly half our time is spent with our thoughts elsewhere, playing out an imaginary scenario in our minds!

Much of the research into daydreaming concludes that it's fundamentally a colossal waste of time, resulting in poor attention, reduced productivity and even with a potential negative impact on our mental health, if we're dreaming of undesirable scenarios. And, on the face of it, yes, daydreaming could be seen as a pesky time thief. You zone out and don't hear something important someone is telling you (rude), you miss your stop on the bus (annoying), you fail to get your work done on time (problematic). But if we all spend so long doing it on the regular, there must be a more positive and useful reason why, and other research has looked into what those potential benefits might be. (To make you feel better about your eyes-open day naps, daydreaming or mind-wandering even has a fancy scientific name: task-unrelated images and thoughts, or TUITS. So next time you find yourself lost in a reverie staring out the window, remember that you are part of a well-considered strand of psychological research.)

Daydreaming has been of interest since at least the 1950s, when Jerome L. Singer was at the forefront of daydream research. His 1975 study divided daydreaming into three separate categories:

positive constructive daydreaming
characterised by playful, wishful imagery, and planful, creative thought

guilty-dysphoric daydreaming
characterised by obsessive, anguished fantasies

poor attentional control
characterised by the inability to concentrate on either the ongoing thought or the external task

In short, there are good and bad daydreams. Bad, unhelpful daydreams are those that see you recalling the past too often, going over that fight with your ex and imagining all the things you could have said. It sees you ruminating and obsessing, leading to nowhere but frustration. Good daydreaming, in contrast, is often linked to our personal goals and the future. Daydreaming is, by its nature, very private and personal – just as our aims in life are – and visualising those goals or playing out potential scenarios in our minds can help us practise for when they become a reality. Keeping your daydreams a little bit grounded in reality means they can become useful tools for life. But that's not to say your daydreams need only involve interactions with your bank manager . . . Daydreaming is also a wonderful, totally free method of escapism and fantasy: Singer described people who take part in positive constructive daydreaming as 'happy daydreamers', with abundant interpersonal curiosity, and who enjoy fantasy, vivid imagery and future planning.

It also seems that daydreaming activates lots of different parts of the brain, allowing us to retrieve information and memories that we may not have thought about in a while. It can allow the mind to make connections between information in ways you may not have considered before. This sounds familiar! We know that connecting ideas in new ways is the route to improved creativity, problem solving and novelty! (See pages 46 and 46.)

So, it turns out daydreaming can be productive after all. It can ignite your imagination and motivate you to follow your dreams. It can also allow you to take a mental break from the task at hand, which can actually be very refreshing for your mind and body. It may even help provide insight on past events and troubling issues, and it can encourage you to 'wander around' your creative brain. In fact, one study showed that daydreamers performed 41 per cent better on creative thinking tests than those who rejected this escapist pastime.

Although it's true that daydreaming may cause you obvious and irritating lapses in concentration, lost seconds and missed information, those moments you spent elsewhere could have been just what you needed to provide insight into a longstanding niggling problem, perspective on a past encounter or your next brilliant new idea.

How to have a good daydream

Don't ruminate on past failures, wishing you'd said that one killer line. Instead, focus on the future, and keep your daydreams more or less in reality. This can help you practise for scenarios that are likely to come up as you move towards your goals and, like in the Law of Attraction (see page 120), imagining circumstances may even help manifest them into your life. Visualise all the details, and play out different scenarios, honing your aims and their positive outcomes.

Listen to your daydreams. Are you constantly dreaming of being anywhere but here, of packing up a suitcase and running away? It doesn't take a psychologist to work out what's going on. It's probably time to make some changes . . . (See page 154 for some ideas.)

Give yourself the time and space to daydream. Mostly, daydreaming is spontaneous – that's sort of its calling card – it's unrelated to what we're *supposed* to be doing. But it is possible to get yourself into a daydream state by being relaxed and allowing your mind to wander as it wills. Lie back and watch the clouds drift by . . . If you can't get your mind to soft-focus, begin by thinking about a random object – an orange, a trophy cup, a woolly jumper – and then see where you end up . . .

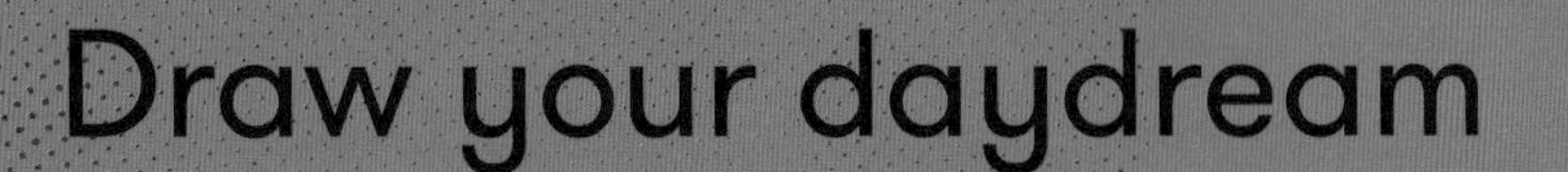

Draw your daydream

Guide yourself through a daydream. Consider each prompt below, and then draw in each space on the comic strip to tell the story of your daydreaming adventure.

Close your eyes. Take yourself to a safe, secure, happy place somewhere outside in nature. What is the ground like? What is the weather like? What is the scenery like?

What does the path look like? How does the scenery change on your walk? Is it flat or hilly? What do you pass on your way?

You come to a wood. What can you hear? Are there lots of trees or can you see the sky above? Are there any animals or birds? What season is it?

You keep walking and come through to the other side of the wood. You see a body of water up ahead – what is it? A pond? A river? The sea? A waterfall?

Nearby, you spot a dwelling – it's your home. What is it like? Does it have a garden? Look at the details of the building. What are the windows like? What colour is the front door?

You zoom up into the sky – what is the surrounding area like? Is your home in the middle of nowhere or are you part of a group of houses? Are there any landmarks nearby?

You enter your house and wander around inside. Which room is your favourite? Why? What does it look like? What can you see?

There's a chair in front of you – what is it like? Sit down. What does it feel like? Close your eyes, and take yourself to a safe, secure place . . .

A playful mind: think fun – how to change your mood when you're not in the mood

It's easy to be fun when you're in the mood for it, or when it's #ThatFridayFeeling, or you're on holiday and the sun's out. It's less easy to master when you have no clean clothes, it's raining for the fifth day in a row, you're exhausted and need a lie-in but it's only Tuesday. Learning how to adopt a more playful attitude during trying times – how to put a playful spin on events, even if only temporarily – is one of the greatest skills play can teach us. Practising a more optimistic outlook means we can call on it during tricky times to help us through.

Say thank you

That current buzzword, gratitude, and the appreciation of the little things can go a long way. Yes, your feet may be wet from the puddles, but how amazing that you're free to walk through them! You're alive! How great that it's raining to water the plants and clean the streets – and doesn't the sky look moody and mysterious when it's dark and stormy? Being able to stay optimistic has plenty of proven benefits for our physical and mental health. From reports that positive people are better at solving problems and less likely to suffer a stroke or heart attack, there is plenty of research into the benefits of adopting a PMA, or Positive Mental Attitude, and seeing the good rather than the bad in situations.

Laughter really is good for us

It's a sad fact that children laugh significantly more often in a day than adults do – a side-splitting 400 times compared with our miserly 15, and I bet some of those are wasted on polite laughs at your co-worker's bad jokes. Apparently the magic number of daily laughs we should be aiming for is 30. Brain mapping has shown it takes the whole brain working as one to process a joke, with the left side setting it up and the right side 'getting' it. So as well as just being enjoyable, laughter can increase cognitive dexterity, which can in turn stimulate creativity and imagination and create new neural pathways . . . all with huge benefits in many aspects of our lives.

Don't let your emotions rule

OK, so we know patience can wear a bit thin for that person who is cheery and positive all of the time. But it is possible to have a little more control over your moods. Your emotions are *you*, so in theory you can learn to manage them rather than have them dominate you. Taking a deep breath before complaining about something can change how you feel about it. So next time you feel a negative thought incoming, try to turn it on its head – see the silver lining rather than the cloud.

Note: Mood disorders such as anxiety or depression are more complex. If dark moods are making life difficult, get expert help.

Change your mood, whatever the weather

Be enthusiastic and positivity will follow you. These activities are for when you just don't feel fun.

Take a moonwalk

Use this simple meditation technique to give yourself some fresh perspective and get you out of that nothing-is-going-right, frustrated mood. Sit on a chair with your feet flat on the floor. In your mind, step outside your body. Look down from the top of your head. Mentally zoom out so you're above your building, what can you see? Zoom out further, above your surrounding area. Keep going, zooming out further and further, above your city – see the tiny cars and people like dots – then your country . . . Keep going until you're bouncing around on the moon looking down at Earth. Take a deep breath and realise that none of this really matters. Now float back down to the ground.

Stop your mood in its tracks

If you're about to say something negative – stop. Don't say it. Negativity leads to more negativity. Say something positive instead.

Watch a comedy animal compilation

If ever the internet was made for a moment, it's watching a cat that thinks a cucumber is a snake or a dog singing with its owner.

Are you in control or not? Feel no fear!

If you're not in a playful mood, there's usually a reason. Losing your shit over a missed bus is likely not about the bus. Why are things getting to you? The opposite of feeling playful is feeling fearful, so what is making you fearful? Once you've worked out the real reason you're in a bitchy mood, what can you do about it? If you can't do anything about your situation, learn to accept it and move on. Once you free your mind from worrying about something you can't do anything about – or tackle a problem head on and solve it – you can use that magical brain space for something more enriching. (See page 222 for ideas to boost your energy; see overleaf for how to sort your shit.)

Find your Positive Pollys

Positive Pollys are those sparkling people in your life who always manage to give you a boost. Create a WhatsApp group of the Positive Pollys you know. No Negative Nellies allowed! Call them, message them or just remind yourself that they are in your life whenever you're heading down a pessimism spiral.

Sorting your shit out

Being playful takes a certain amount of carefreeness. Sometimes 'fake it till you make it' does the trick and being playful will make you carefree. But sometimes, if you find you've lost your playfulness, it may be because there really are things on your mind that you need to deal with, or because you're letting your time run away with you and not taking charge of allocating your 'play' time.

Sometimes it's not even clear why your life isn't as playful as it should be. If you find yourself here, you gotta get serious about making your life playful. You gotta sort your shit out.

But how? And isn't that what we're trying to do all the time anyway? Well, yes. Sometimes it's not easy. For me, when I find my playfulness is low, the first thing I need to do is take a look at how I'm spending my time. Am I letting it roll by and get swallowed up without any clear conscious intention on my part? Are other people dictating it? By taking charge of the time you *need* to spend doing things – work, commitments, chores – you're better able to plan in things that are fun, which means that you are able to be completely 'off' during those times so you can really let go and have fun. And who doesn't love a colour-coded, hourly time-blocked week-to-view to feel a sense of control and peace? I highly recommend time-blocking your life, not just your work. Knowing you've got down everything you need to do with enough time to do it frees you up to enjoy it so much more.

If you've never time-blocked before, start by spending a few weeks filling in your diary retrospectively. I like using an electronic diary so I can drag things around. At the end of the working day I fill in what I actually did for every hour, then the next morning I fill in the evening gaps – apart from sleeping and showering. The first time you do this it can be quite a shock to see how wildly different your estimates of how long things take are compared to how long you actually spent doing them. We tend to overestimate the time spent doing the things we don't enjoy and underestimate how long we spend doing the enjoyable stuff. Added to that, our concept of how quickly time moves changes day to day. I often use the timer on my electric toothbrush to see how my brain is measuring time; sometimes it seems to take forever to go off, other times it turns itself off before I've even got to my bottom teeth.

'Life isn't as serious as my mind makes it to be.'
Eckhart Tolle

After a couple of weeks you can look back and see how much time you actually spend doing different things, then block out your routine tasks. Putting things into an automatic routine saves brainpower, which can then be freed up for playful thoughts. You might even come up with ways to make these routine jobs more enjoyable.

OK, now for the next step in sorting your shit out. Plan some alone time. That doesn't sound very playful, does it? It's not – this is serious introspection and reflection time.

What's killing your fun?

1

Diary block an hour. Let anyone who might steal this time know you have an important meeting with yourself and it can't be rescheduled or interrupted.

2

Get a pen and a notebook (or find some paper) so you've got two blank pages in front of you.

3

Shut yourself off from anything that demands your attention. Read these instructions when you're ready to do it; if necessary bookmark them and come back.

4

Set a timer for five minutes – if you have to use your phone it must be in airplane mode!

5

Wait for the timer in total silence.

6

Write down every thought you can remember from the silence. If some thoughts looped round, make this clear by writing it over again or marking with 'x 10'. Keep writing for the full two pages. Get all the chatter in your head down on paper, writing as fast as you can. You don't have to read it back and no one else will ever see it. If you have some particularly pertinent thoughts or things you want to remember later, write them tidily or make a bullet list so your brain can let go of them.

7

Now set the timer for 10 minutes.

8

Now take a more conscious observation of your thoughts. Do things come up that you've already put on paper and could be free from for the rest of the hour? Think about why it might be that you aren't resting them there. Has this made space for different thoughts to reveal themselves? If the first roaming of your mind was a work to-do list is it now life chores? Are you replaying things that happened in the past? Are you worrying or dreaming about things yet to come? There's no right answer here or 'bad' way for your thoughts to be.

9

Write all these thoughts down. Include what the thoughts were AND your reflections about the thoughts. Write continuously to fill these pages. Don't reread or pause for thought. Just keep the pen moving. As you write do you have more reflections? Get them down too. How did those 10 minutes of introspection feel? Did it fly while you were dreaming or did it stretch for a cold long eternity? Answers on a postcard.

10

Hopefully your head is clearer now. Reset that timer for 10 minutes. This time bring your conscious awareness to how you *feel*. You can start with how you feel physically. Are there aches? Have your legs gone dead while you've been sitting here? Is your nose cold? (My nose is always cold.) How does your breath feel in your chest. Is your stomach comfortable? I like to think of my neck as my body's 'direct dial', telling my conscious mind what my gut and heart is telling me. Open your attention so you can listen to this without premeditating what you'll find.

11

Guess what's coming next? Yup, you gotta write them all down.

12

Scan back at your thoughts. Are they facts? Could there be other ways of seeing them? Are these worth your precious time?

13

Look at your feelings. They are all wholly valid and true. Are they disrupting your playful, joyful life? What is the cause of these? Is it past situations that need healing so you can move forward? Or are they present situations that you need to take action to change?

the success of failure

Climbing up the big slide in the park taught you many things. As you executed that scary manoeuvre at the top, with everyone watching you from below, you learned that you could do it! As you teetered at the very pinnacle of the world, you saw it from a whole new perspective – with you as its master.

These days adventure playgrounds aren't such a common part of childhood as they used to be. They're often seen as unsafe, or they're not well looked after, or else they're dismantled and the land used for something else. Meanwhile, we're seeing a generation of children grow up more anxious than ever. Is there a link?

Testing our abilities, taking calculated risks, getting back up and trying again – it's these real-life experiences that show us what we can achieve, what we're capable of and where we need to try again or take a different approach. Play is a great no-pressure way to experiment and practise failing. It doesn't really matter if you don't succeed – if you miss a shot at goal or your pottery sculpture blows up in the kiln. It's disappointing, sure. But then you'll also learn to deal with disappointments – and as we know, life tends to have a few of these in store for us, so it's best to be prepared.

Trying things out allows us to learn about our physical and mental skills, strengths and weaknesses. And it also lets us reframe how we view failure. Sir James Dyson made more than 5,000 prototypes of his vacuum cleaner before he found the one that was the winner: that's more than 5,000 failures before he found success. When things don't work, they show you where you need to improve. Hardly anyone gets it right first time.

'Play is training for the unexpected.'
Marc Bekoff

Being a bit braver and 'giving it a go' can open up a whole new world for us. The more we practise being brave, the less scary things will start to seem. Remember when something seemed like the most daunting thing ever? And now we do it without a second thought? Testing yourself without there being any major consequences can build your confidence and bravery for when it really matters.

Obviously, don't take uncalculated or stupid risks that are going to place you in danger or risk you losing all your money, friends and future prospects. But think about the small ways you can be a bit bolder in your everyday. Work out what your mental monkey bars are and take that first swing at them.

5-minute ideas for everyday bravery

How often do we all feel like telling our younger selves to be a bit braver, to take a few more risks, to live in the now a bit more? Well, be your older self telling your younger self that today.

Try a new food

Being brave can be as simple as trying something different. And once you start trying new things, there'll be no stopping you. (See also page 154 for ways to shake up your routine.)

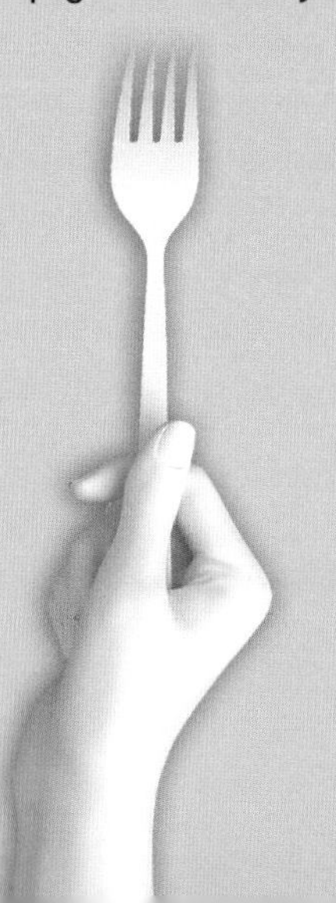

Phone someone instead of texting

This seems ridiculous, but how many of us now jump when our phone rings? Have a real conversation and you'll also reap the benefits of social interaction too (see page 72).

Speak up at a meeting

Speak up with an idea that might be good, or to point out when someone has got it wrong. Speaking out shows people who you are – you're not to be messed with. You're no wallflower.

Ask for help

Often, being brave is about feeling safe and supported by the people around you, so you can feel confident about taking a risk. There's nothing braver than saying 'I'm scared about this, please support me.' But know that pretty much everyone will say yes. Start small and build up slowly.

Smile at a stranger, say hello to your local shopkeeper

It's nice to feel connected to people around us – we're all the same really, muddling along in more or less the same way – so don't close yourself off from those around you. (See page 72 for the benefits of connecting with people around you.)

Step out of your style

Try a bright red lipstick if you're usually a pink girl, some Pat Butcher earrings or a jazzy

top and trouser combo. It can feel massively brave wearing something bold and outside your regular go-tos, but everyone else either won't even notice how fabulous you look, or else will send big compliments your way.

Push your physical bravery

This is a more immediate and tangible way of testing your limits. Try a new sport or class. Sign up for yoga – even if you can't touch your toes. There's nothing more supportive and welcoming than a beginner's yoga class! (See also page 240 for an at-home yoga sequence and beginner's parkour on page 250.)

Thinking visually

Mostly we go about our day using words – we tend to think in words, we use verbal language to communicate, we write lists. Unless we are a visual artist spending blissful days in the studio, most of us neglect our visual-thinking skills. But that's not to say we aren't instinctive visual thinkers; it's a major part of how we interpret and interact with the modern world. Our phones use symbols – we click on all those little colourful 'buttons' – we love an emoji, we are obsessed with Instagram.

We know we daydream (see page 162) and dream at night (see page 206), so we are perfectly able to think visually. Some people think almost exclusively in a visual way – seeing words and ideas as images. But most use a combination of verbal and visual thinking.

Practising thinking more visually is an instantly more playful and imaginative way to approach and navigate the world around us. It forces us to notice colours and shapes, and to interact more physically and viscerally with our environment. Getting better at visual thinking can result in improved creativity, and can help you understand difficult ideas more easily.

When we can visualise an idea or a problem (drawing our thoughts on paper or using a diagram to explain a concept, for example) we can work through its processes step by step.

This way, you can literally 'see' your way through to the solution and it can help you picture how a finished project will look. When you draw something, your thoughts are able to go in different directions much more easily, too – think spider diagrams shooting off across the page in an unconstrained fashion, not lists running downwards in an orderly A to B. See also the benefits of doodling on pages 24–26.

Thinking visually throughout the week

Let's make the effort to consciously look around us and interact with and interpret our environment in a more visually engaged way. Conduct entire conversations via the hieroglyphics of our modern times: the emoji. Plan a date, arrange a meeting or discuss your feelings on a hot topic or your views on the latest film or political scandal using only sequences of those tiny pics. Schedule events in your diary using pictures. Keep a track of your moods.

Want to let someone know you're thinking about them? Draw a picture of them and send it to them with love – either in the post or take a snap on your phone and ping it over for instant gratification.

Picture this . . .

A classic visual thinking test is to task people to turn 100 circles into something else. You can link several together or treat them in isolation. The more imaginative the better.

EXPERT IN PLAY

TRISTAN WILLIAMS, JOINT FOUNDER OF BIG POTATO GAMES

Board games to the rescue

When was the last time you discovered that your gran knew what Tinder was? Or that your dad would happily abandon you on a dying planet? Or that your best friend thought your middle name was Ian?

Well, when was the last time you played a board game?

Here at Big Potato we make board games that are easy to learn, quick to play and, most importantly of all, make people laugh, celebrate, get competitive, say silly things and do the unexpected. Something magical happens when a group of friends become engrossed in a good game. They forget everything else that's going on in the world for 30 minutes and they just enjoy each other's company.

But sometimes something remarkable happens. Shy people become extroverts, serious people hilarious, and cautious people turn into outrageous risk-takers. Board games allow us to come out of our shell without embarrassment – after all, we can just blame it on the game!

And the good news is, there has never been a better time to buy a board game than today. Gone are the days when it was just a choice of Buckaroo or Kerplunk in the local toy shop. Now you can pick from hundreds of truly innovative titles that will catapult you to Mars, send you into the deep in a submarine or get you to throw burritos at each other.

When I founded Big Potato back in 2013 with my two pals, Dean and Ben, board games were still clinging on to past glories. The industry felt a bit old-fashioned and set in its ways. We saw an opportunity to bring some much-needed fun and colour to the party, and while we can't claim to be the driving force behind the golden age of board games that we're living through now, hopefully we played a part in it.

As child I always loved board games, reinventing rules to classics and even inventing my own. But unless one of the big game companies were interested, your idea was destined to live in the bottom drawer. But now everything has changed. Crowdfunding sites mean small inventors can reach the masses, Amazon means they can set up their own shops and even the big boys like Hasbro, Spinmaster and Mattel are actively looking for indie titles to take on.

We really are living through the golden age of board games, and thank heavens for that, because we could all do with a laugh, couldn't we?

DON'T GET GOT!

o Get a player to correct your pronunciation of something.	o Get a player's birthday wrong and get them to correct you.
o Get a player to say 'You're wrong.'	o Get a player to try to cure your hiccups.
o Get a player to fist-bump you twice in one day.	o Get a player to make an animal noise.
o Say a player's name just slightly wrong and get them to correct you.	o Pick an object and tell a player that it smells really weird. Get them to smell it.
o Drop something and get a player to pick it up for you.	o Get a player to say 'Game over'.
o Get a player to make a fart noise.	o Get a player to cut a label off the clothes you're wearing.

Get them before they get you

Here is a sample of our game called Don't Get Got. It's not your sit-down-at-table sort of game, you play it while doing other things and going about your day. Cut out the missions, divvy them up and the person who completes the most (without getting caught) wins. Enjoy.

o Get a player to make a deer noise by telling them that deer don't make noises.	o Balance on one leg and wait for a player to try to push you over.
o Get a movie quote wrong and get another player to correct you.	o Get a player to play Rock-Paper-Scissors with you (until you win).
o Get a player to lie down on the floor with you.	o Get a player to tie a knot for you.
o Throw a paper airplane at a player and get them to throw it back at you.	o Get a player to read a sentence from a book out loud.
o Suggest a song and get another player to play it on their phone.	o Insist that an actor in a film is someone else and get a player to check on the internet.

Object

To be the first player to successfully complete three of your missions

Set up

Cut out or write out the mission cards on pages 186–87, or come up with some of your own. Deal five random mission cards to each player, facedown.

How to play

There is no time limit to this game. It ends when a player completes three missions or when everyone runs out of missions to complete.

Completing a mission

Each mission involves tricking a player in some way. If you manage to successfully pull off a mission, show that player your mission card. Make sure you let all the other players know that you're one step closer to victory!

Failing a mission

If any player calls you out before you complete your mission, your mission has failed. It's off-limits for the rest of the game.

Example

If might go something like this – you pretend that you can't open a jar of jam and you hand it to another player asking if they can help. Without thinking, they take it, open the lid, and find your card inside: 'Hide this card in a jar. Get a player to open it'. You've got them! However, if the player smells a rat and won't open the jar, accusing you of trying to trick them, then you just come clean. You've failed that mission.

Hide this card in a jar.
Get a player to open it.

Tips

- Never let your guard down. The game is always on until someone wins.

- Most of these missions are purposely open, so you'll need to get creative to complete them.

- Keep score by creating a message channel with all the other players and share pics of your victims whenever you complete a mission.

- You can play this game while playing another game of doing other things. It's designed to run in the background.

SURPRISE!

Spontaneity is thought to be one of the main characteristics shared by innovative thinkers. Dr K. H. Kim, a Professor of Creativity and Innovation, believes that for many people, over-thinking a situation can prevent them coming up with a solution or taking action, whereas a spontaneous attitude leads to more flexible decision-making.

She also throws in the words 'chaotic thinking' – in a good way . . .

We've all experienced that feeling of weighing up the pros and cons for so long we don't know what the answer is any more and all our ideas seem terrible. In work goals, just as in life and creative endeavours, we could all do with taking more action sometimes, hiding less behind our planning, spreadsheets and lists and just taking a chance and seeing where we end up. Sometimes it's only in the doing that we can figure out what works for us and what definitely does not.

To be a successful innovator, overflowing with creative and forward-thinking ideas, we need to encourage spontaneity and flexible thinking. We need to let those ideas flow freely, without limits. OK, so not all of them will be great (although no bad ideas in brainstorming, right?), but we need to let them surface unrestricted. Dr Kim says that what should follow this ideas-generation session is a little break, a daydream (see page 162) or just some easy, non-taxing work – or maybe even a quick nap? The final, very important step is to critically analyse those ideas later, evaluating them for their usefulness. This clever combination of spontaneity and persistence is what she believes is the root of successful innovative thinking.

> 'A little fun can go a long way to making your work feel like play'
> Julia Cameron

Improvisational jazz is one of the best examples of spontaneous creativity. A John Hopkins study into the brains of jazz musicians found that when they are in full improvisational flow the areas associated with planning, self-censoring and inhibition were switched off, while those allowing self-expression, individuality and creativity were turned on. They concluded the process of improv jazz '[shuts] down impulses that might impede the flow of novel ideas'. They even suggest that this creative spontaneity is integral to the advancement of the human species – that's quite a claim! It's this kind of quick-thinking, creative improvisation that we need to solve problems and be adaptable to change.

Grab life by the horns

Being spontaneous is about seeing the opportunities around you and taking advantage of them. It's about being open to experiences, allowing a small spark of an idea to grow in whatever direction it wants. It's also about trusting in yourself. To take risks and plunge into things without too much planning requires you to have some faith that everything will be OK in the end. The trick is to have confidence that either things will work out, or if they don't, then it's not that things haven't gone right, it's that you have learned something new.

Remember that everything has brought you to where you are right now – you have an enormous amount of experience already, so learn to trust in that a bit more. The more playfully spontaneous you are and the more risks you take, the more you'll have confidence that things will work out again next time too. You'll have less fear because you know you were absolutely fine last time – more than fine – you thrived and got a thrill from whatever spontaneous action you took! Leave yourself open to chance opportunities and act more on impulse.

Over-planning, detailed scheduling and thinking too much about every possible outcome kills off spontaneity. But being cautious is a very sensible survival instinct, so spontaneity may not always come naturally. To ease yourself into spontaneous thinking, try leaving decision-making to an element of chance. Then once you feel comfortable with the idea that one option probably isn't really any worse than any other, listen to your instincts and take that leap.

Flip a coin

Our old friend the coin: heads for yes; tails for no; heads for tuna mayo baguette; tails for falafel wrap.

Thumb war

A battle of strength between two players – who goes to make the tea this time?

Rock, paper, scissors

The ultimate in housemate task assignment, who does a snack run or what series to binge.

Origami fortune teller

For more complex decisions or those with multiple possible solutions, make a paper decision maker – for up to eight impromptu, magical answers. The original magic eight-ball.

Free up your mind: remove choice

The flip side to keeping things interesting, to experimenting with new routines, to practising spontaneity (is that an oxymoron?) and trying out unchartered paths is to restrict all choices and decision-making down to the absolute minimum. Barack Obama was famous for wearing the same blue or black suits every day when he was in office, and Mark Zuckerberg is synonymous with his unimaginative jeans-and-T-shirt combo.

Our brains don't really distinguish between the anguish of what sandwich to buy at lunch and whether or not we should move to Canada, treating each with more or less the same level of dedication. And the more decisions we make throughout the day, the worse we get at it. Psychologists call this decision fatigue.

In order to free up that amazing creative brain of yours to focus on more exciting endeavours – to help you solve that million-dollar problem or develop a brilliant new idea – try paring things right down. Plan your meals ahead, choose a quick capsule wardrobe for the week, decide now that you won't drink until Friday. It's important not to let ALL aspects of your life become Groundhog Day. But without all those hundreds of mundane decisions we have to make on a day-to-day basis, think of all the extra brain space you can fill with other more experimental thoughts?!

Get militant with your diary

This may sound like the absolute opposite of a playful, carefree approach to life, but compartmentalising your time can be the key to freeing up your mind! Try the time-blocking exercise on page 173 or divide up your week into blocks for regular meetings, work tasks, downtime and creative thinking time. Plan in relaxation, schedule those yoga classes, gym sessions or stroking your dog time – whatever it is that keeps you grounded. Book in that bubble bath on a Friday night so you're not burnt out, plan in whatever it is you need to stop yourself feeling overloaded and stretched in a million directions. You can even colour-code it if you like – work, exercise, creative projects, turn-my-phone-off-and-don't-talk-to-anyone time. Be disciplined, and allow proper, quality time for each event. Doing this will mean you'll always be present, fully engaged and feeling relaxed and more playful because you know that everything is covered – you may not remember exactly what you're doing on Thursday at 2pm, but it's in the diary so it's all sorted – you can stop worrying about when you'll have time to get to the bank/finish that project/get your eyebrows done because it's all factored in.

Doing some of the same things at the same time each week can also mean you don't have to constantly think 'where am I supposed to be?!', reducing anxiety and those sweaty feelings of being out of control. You can even block out some diary planning time into your diary. It may sound the most uncreative approach to creativity and playfulness, but try it – if you set aside some proper time to play and daydream, knowing that that's all you are meant to be doing at that moment, you'll relax into it and get fully involved. It's all about ying and yang, innit?

EXPERT IN PLAY

PROFESSIONAL PUZZLER DR GARETH MOORE

Dr Gareth Moore is the author of over 100 best-selling puzzle and brain-training books. Find out more at DrGarethMoore.com.

Puzzles are fun, but did you know that they can also benefit you? Your brain loves to learn, and that includes the skills you'll need to solve a sudoku, crack a cryptogram or work out a word search. What's more, you learn best while you're relaxed and at ease, so the natural fun and enjoyment of the puzzle-solving process also grants you a free top-up on the mental benefits.

The best mental gains come from trying something new, so it's lucky that there are hundreds of different types of puzzle. It's tempting to stick to what you already know, but you'll get the greatest benefit – and possibly discover a new favourite – by tackling puzzles you haven't tried before. And, what's more, the process of experimentation could even help your brain learn to assist with better decision-making in other aspects of your life too.

Sometimes our lives feel overrun with distractions, which is one way in which the focus required to solve a puzzle can come in handy. You won't make much headway with the average crossword or sudoku unless you're properly concentrating, so next time you need a break you could do much worse than to pick up a pencil and start solving.

Sometimes it's good just to clear your mind and forget about work for a while, and it might even help you improve your wellbeing, since long-term stress isn't good for your grey matter.

It's easy to think of keeping fit as something that mainly affects the bits of your body you can see, but keeping your brain healthy is the most important thing of all – since without it, what would you be? Making good use of your thinking abilities is a key part of this, and the oft-quoted maxim 'use it or lose it' is scarily close to the money. Your brain will, quite literally, discard thinking circuits that you no longer use, which is just one of many reasons why it's important to make sure you don't pass your days in a drudgery of unchallenging tasks. What we don't know, however, is exactly which activities will provide the best mental benefits, so tackling the widest range of puzzles and other challenges you can find is simply the safest course.

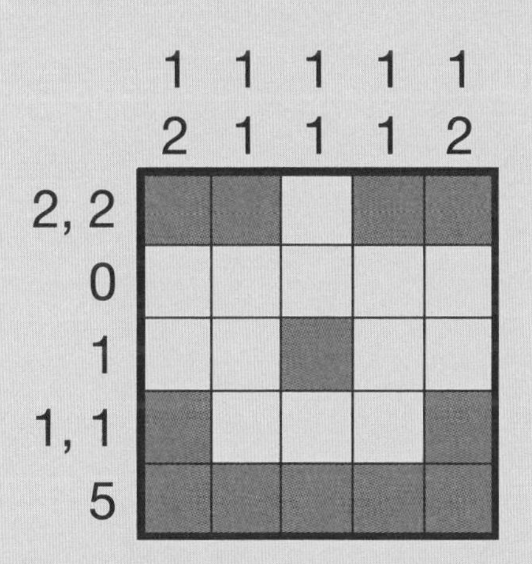

Developing new ways of thinking, as your brain works out how to tackle new types of puzzle, is good in itself – but puzzles are designed to be solvable so you'll also get that little mental kick of success when you finish a challenge. Your brain loves this mental pat on the back, which is one reason why sudoku is so successful: people love filling in all the boxes! Somehow, if you can complete a puzzle, other tasks in life don't seem *quite* so daunting to your brain. And, what's more, that little burst of joy you get when you finish a puzzle can also help calm your mind, in much the same way that physical exercise can mentally relax you too.

The range of skills required to solve a puzzle even extends beyond the direct mental challenge. Sometimes in life it can be hard to take the very first step when starting something new, so the practice of doing so successfully on a much less critical task can help you nudge yourself into a more positive mindset. After all, if that impenetrable grid of symbols has fallen to your mental prowess, then other tasks may turn out to be just a bit more manageable than you had previously thought.

New types of puzzle are being invented all the time, yet it would take a lifetime to master those that exist already – so it's never too soon to start your puzzle odyssey! You could begin, if you wish, by tackling the following two 'hanjie' puzzles. Each of them will even grant you a bonus burst of satisfaction on completion, too, since both puzzles solve to reveal simple pictures.

Hanjie puzzle

The rules are simple: shade some squares to match the clues outside the grid. Each clue provides, in reading order, the length of every run of consecutive shaded cells in its row or column. There must be a gap of at least one empty cell between each run of shaded cells in the same row or column. Take a look at the solved example on the previous page to see how this works.

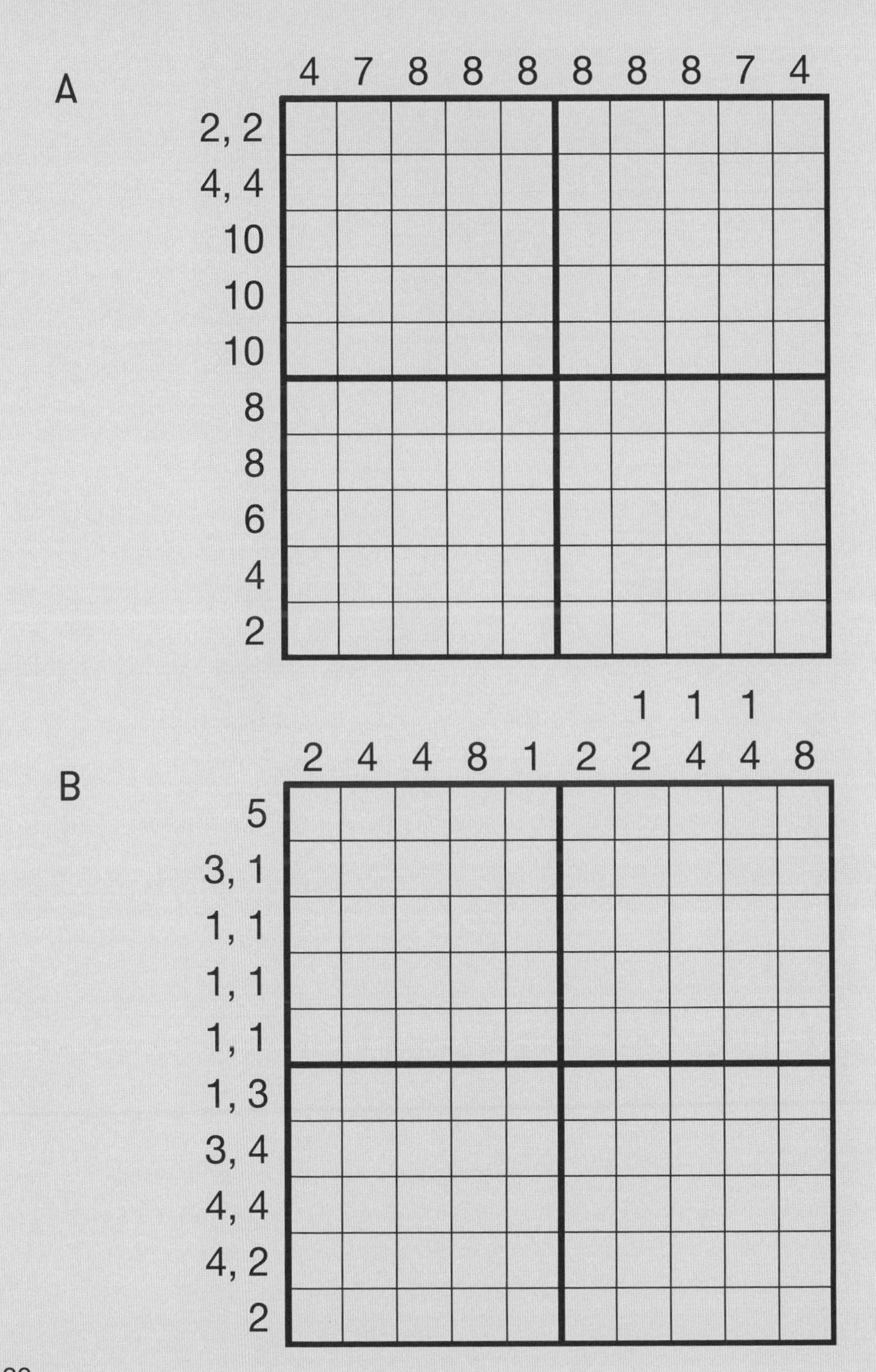
A
4 7 8 8 8 8 8 8 7 4
2, 2
4, 4
10
10
10
8
8
6
4
2
B
1 1 1
2 4 4 8 1 2 2 4 4 8
5
3, 1
1, 1
1, 1
1, 1
1, 3
3, 4
4, 4
4, 2
2

Meditation and creative thinking

Many of the world's most successful people meditate (from Oprah to the CEO of Twitter) and there's solid science to back up why this might be. It has been proven to help with anxiety, sleep issues and our general wellbeing, but did you know it can actually rewire your brain?

Meditation has been shown to increase your focus, attention, memory and creativity, and it also helps you find your state of flow.

Studies of Buddhist monks, for whom meditation is a regular part of their daily routine, show evidence of high plasticity of the brain, meaning their brains are more capable of change and resilience.

Meditation has also been shown to increase empathy. In one study, a subject described his meditation as generating 'a state in which love and compassion permeate the whole mind.' The thinking behind this is that our brains run on two systems – the extrinsic network, which is activated when we are focused on external tasks, and the intrinsic or default network, which is concerned with our emotions and reflection. Throughout our day these networks are active to different degrees, depending on what we are doing. But it has been found that Buddhist monks and other regular meditation practitioners are able to keep both these networks active at the same time during meditation. Dr Josipovic, who conducted this research, believes this is why monks experience such an intense harmonious sense of oneness with their environment.

It is thought that meditation slows down our reptilian brain and instead stimulates the neocortex, which is where creative thinking thrives. Research has also shown that non-meditators are more rigid in their thinking – which as we know is the opposite of what we need to be as freethinking creative innovators!

However, it seems that certain types of meditation may be more beneficial to creative thinking than others. Focused attention (FA) meditation requires you to concentrate on a single object, mantra, sound or body part. Your aim is to stop your mind wandering and to tune out any outside distractions. By contrast, open monitoring (OM) meditation allows for your attention to be open to whatever is going on around you – whether that's your own thoughts and memories that surface, or bodily sensations or events in your environment. But rather than fully engage with these experiences, you simply witness them – as though you're watching a film of them playing out inside your head.

It is OM meditation that has been shown to have a positive effect on creativity and helps to foster divergent thinking. There is some (although less solid) evidence to support the idea that FA meditation supports convergent thinking – the process involved in puzzling out one solution to a specific problem. So the type of meditation that will benefit your thinking could depend on what you want to achieve.

Another good thing about OM meditation is that you don't need to be particularly experienced in it to see the effects. Buddhist monks often have thousands of hours of meditation under their belts, but it's refreshing to know you could start today and still see a positive effect on your creativity.

Get your OM on

Mindfulness meditation, which has been a buzzword in the wellness sector for ages, actually utilises both OM and FA meditation: you focus on one activity, object or sensation, but you leave yourself open to your outside environment too.

The great thing about mindfulness meditation is that you can do it anywhere – while you eat your morning toast, on the bus, in the dentist's waiting room – you can even do active mindfulness meditation while you're hoovering the stairs. There are plenty of apps you can download to guide you through your first foray into meditation, but soon you'll be able to do it wherever you are.

The best way to make meditation part of your everyday is to include it as part of your daily activities. Like when you eat your lunch: rather than skimming emails, news sites or eating on the move, sit down (it can even be at your desk if you must) and just eat that salad and be fully in the moment – how does it look, how does it smell and taste, what are those textures like, how hungry are you, how do you feel as you eat it? Observe these thoughts, then move on to the next bite. When other things pop up in your mind, acknowledge them, then get back to that salad. Keep your breathing calm and your brain will follow.

Guided meditation

Close your eyes and start to listen to the sounds you can hear. Start with the loudest ones, the most obvious ones, acknowledge each in turn, then look for a smaller one. When you think you have run out of sounds, listen more carefully. Listen for sounds closer to you. Listen until you can hear yourself breathe. If you can't hear your breath you can breathe a bit more loudly until you can focus on it.

After a few minutes focusing on your breath, or maybe counting to thirty breaths without breaking your concentration, start to shift your concentration to the sound of your breath from your outside ears to the sound of your breath inside your head. In this way we use our breath to shift our experience from the outside world to our inside world. Notice the little pauses between the inhale and exhale.

Watch the breath move the body without effort. Observe where the body is moving a lot. Up in the chest or the sides of the ribcage? How much is the belly moving? In this relaxed breath the belly should be lifting as you inhale and softening as you exhale. When we force the breath, the belly may be sucked in as we inhale. Try to watch this and soften the effort.

Start to notice where else the body is being moved by the breath. Visualise the breath as gentle waves lapping at a shore;

the waves reaching further and further, so you are experiencing your breath all the way through your body.

As your mind is focused on the sensations of the body, scan through your muscles and joints. How are they feeling? Does one side feel different to the other? Is there any pain or tightness? Make sure you're not passing a negative judgement on anything you do find. You're just looking with an abstract detachment, just seeing what is really there without a story behind why it's annoying you. Don't try to fix anything.

Your body is just right as it is here today. It's carried you to this point and you're in exactly the right place and it's in exactly the right condition.

Once you've finished patiently exploring the inside sensations of the physical body, notice how you are feeling energetically. Is there a buzz of anxious firefly energy that makes stillness difficult? Or is there a lethargic energy that makes it hard to stay awake? There's no right or wrong with how it is right now. It will be different in a few hours' time. There is no 'should be' for this time in the day, or in your life.

Next, watch what is happening with your thoughts. Are there thoughts jumping in, cutting up your focus to your inward observations? How rapidly or how leisurely do they come? What is the nature of these thoughts? What is the weather of your mind like today? Dark and stormy? Bright but blustery? Still with dappled sun?

Now that you've given your mind some proper attention, see if you can go beyond the thoughts to look into the feelings. Not the words and stories of the experiences of your life but the sensation of your gut and of your heart. Everyone carries some hurt and pain. Even those with happy lives have had their own worst thing happen to them. It can be hard for these feelings to surface at first. They are hiding away like a shamed child. Give your feeling some encouragement to come to the tangible levels of your consciousness.

Be a cheerleader for whatever you may find there. Embrace it. Repeat 'yes' to whatever label you may give to the things you find. Fear – yes, yes, yes . . . until you notice another feeling appear.

When we learn a physical skill we are building neural pathways from our brain to our body. The outcome is very clear. We learned to write, throw a ball and drive. When learning to read we do it out loud so we have the guidance and support of others in our learning effort. Looking at letters took some time to understand them, to recognise the sounds and string them together. This is a practice just like that. We're looking. At first the letters may seem like wiggles on the page but slowly we start to recognise the same shape coming up again and again, we begin to recognise it. We begin to accept these feelings as part of us, we make peace with ourselves.

'This is the real secret of life - to be completely engaged with what you are doing in the here and now. And instead of calling it work, realize it is play.'
Alan W Watts

Slowly work your way back through the layers. Go into the thoughts; how are they now? Go back to the energy; what is it now? Experience your physical body again. Notice your clothes against your skin, the weight of your muscles and the support of the earth beneath you. Start to deepen your breath. Breathe all the way down to your fingers and toes and give them a stretch. Take your arms overhead, breathe in a whole-body stretch. Curl yourself in tight, gently start to flicker your eyes open. And go about having a lovely day.

Dreams

We have been recording what we dream for thousands of years – from the wax tablets of Mesopotamia to the dream journals of today. But despite our fascination with our personal nocturnal storytelling, it seems science still isn't in agreement about *why* we dream.

Theories abound, from dreaming being an important process to help us remember events and new information we have learned during the day, to an opportunity to test out future scenarios, or simply random nonsense that our brain plays to stop itself switching off completely.

Two of the most interesting theories of why we dream, however, are to assist in problem-solving and to understand our unconscious self (hello, Mr Freud).

When it comes to problem-solving, our dream-like state is in free-flow – there are no limits – compared with those we impose on ourselves in our waking life. Sometimes this leads to a confused mess of psychedelic uselessness, but at other times it can really help us out of a bind. In one study, 25 per cent of those who focused on a specific problem before they drifted off to sleep managed to solve that problem within a week. That's some pretty impressive night-time problem-solving going on! Famous examples of dream-state creativity include the design of the Pyramid Stage at Glastonbury, and the periodic table. Steinbeck even came up with a name for this effective night-time problem-solving: The Committee of Sleep.

Meanings in dreams are a little more difficult to track. Freud – and others – consider dreams and nightmares to be the manifestation of our subconscious desires. Dreaming links our waking self with our subconscious self. But rather than dreams having specific universal meanings, our individual interpretations should aim to be a little more subjective.

To work out the mysteries of your dreams

- ○ When you wake up, don't get up straight away. Instead, hover in that in-between state on the edge of sleep and try to recall any specific feelings or images from your dreams.
- ○ If you have recurring dreams or nightmares, work out what the key themes are.
- ○ Write them down, or even better draw them – dreaming is visual after all, so sometimes what we dream is better recorded in pictures.
- ○ Then consider how those images, feelings and symbols relate to you personally and whatever you have going on in your life right now.

Common scenarios, such as being chased, could indicate you need to action some change in your situation. Seeing someone in your life as a monster in your dreams is likely to suggest that you don't quite trust them . . . So far, so obvious. But some symbolism is going to be more specific to you – a red car could mean nothing to one person, but to another evokes heart-wrenching memories of their first car, of freedom, and of opportunity and potential that perhaps they are missing today.

'It is a common experience that a problem difficult at night is resolved in the morning after the committee of sleep has worked on it.'
—John Steinbeck

Shape your dreams

Even though the scientific jury is still out on why we dream, it doesn't stop us from looking for hidden meanings! For the next week, draw in each box the main symbols from your night-time dreams and consider what they might mean to you.

Technology and what it's doing to our brains

We now have access to more information than we could ever have imagined possible. What's more, the majority of it is shared freely. It's as though we are working on an enormous group project with worldwide participants all contributing to our collective online memory bank. It's truly amazing – a democratisation of education. But what exactly is it doing to our brains, and is tech ultimately good or evil?

Obviously, the good vs evil debate is not clear-cut – as with most things it comes down to how you use it – but what we do know is that technology is altering how our minds work. We are becoming much more used to accessing bite-sized bits of information; we scan rather than read from start to finish with focused attention – those flashing ads and links to other articles at the side of our screens are constant distractions. We take in vast amounts of information in a more visual way, and we are bombarded with huge quantities of data all the time.

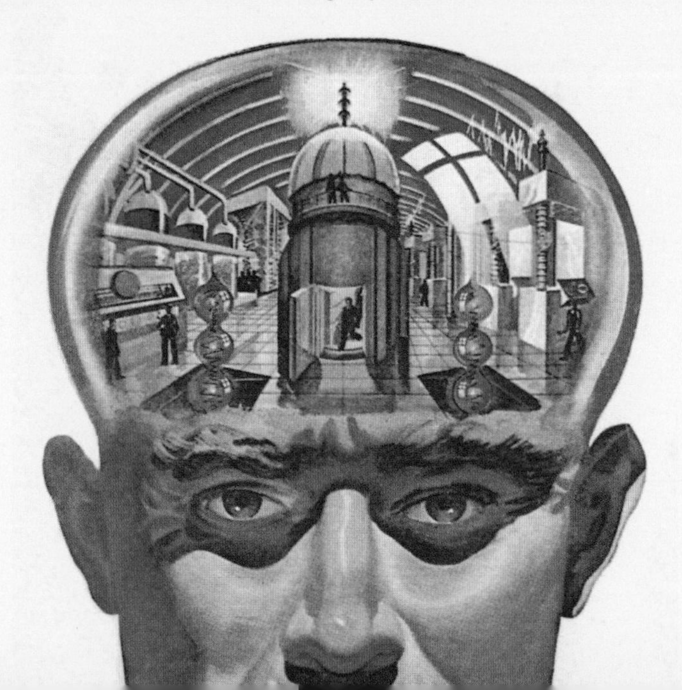

All this extra information and the various platforms through which we constantly communicate are thought to have improved our multi-tasking abilities (check how many tabs you have open on your browser next time you're online), as we learn to switch our attention between answering an email, taking a phone call, or opening a message to watch a baby fall asleep into a cake. But these kinds of endless interruptions and intrusions are also seriously damaging our attention span and our ability to focus on a single task. With so much information accessible even from our phones in our pockets, we are also getting worse at remembering things – online has become our collective memory. Now, we focus more on the skills of *how* to access that information rather than learning it in the first place – but why do we need to? It's right there.

> 'We don't stop playing because we grow old; we grow old because we stop playing.'
> George Bernard Shaw

That constant pinging and buzzing is also playing havoc with our dopamine levels (see page 18). We can start to feel edgy if we haven't checked our phones in a while, needing that 'fix' even while we're in the middle of doing something that we used to enjoy, like reading a book, watching a film or listening to music. Many of us (most of us?) are guilty of checking our phones several times an hour, cycling through emails, messages, social media apps, news feeds, then back round again. We are so addicted, it's often the first thing we check in the morning and the last thing at night, carefully placing our phones by our beds. And we all know it's bad for our sleep.

The influence of tech on our minds is not an entirely recent phenomenon. Studies have found that people who grew up before colour television were much more likely to dream in black and white, whereas younger participants – whose childhoods were shaped by Technicolor – almost always dreamed in colour. However, earlier research suggests that it was the advent of black-and-white television that led people to dream in black and white in the first place. Since our dreams play such an important role in linking our unconscious and conscious selves, perhaps hinting at unresolved issues and our personal goals (see page 206), what influence did this major shift have on our psyches? Is it any wonder the sixties and seventies were psychedelic?!

We often consider emojis to be the downfall of language. But emojis, and in fact the way our technology is designed, with its 'buttons' and 'click on this' links, could actually be improving our visual thinking skills. We have been shown to respond to emojis in a similar way to actual faces showing real emotions, and for many these little smiley/sad/upside-down icons can help communicate often difficult feelings.

Gaming

Playing computer games has often come under attack as an antisocial waste of time, but gaming is huge and on the rise – and it's definitely not just for teenage boys. Computer games now are works of art, combining incredibly high levels of creativity with musical composition and complex storytelling. The worlds that are created are detailed and imaginative, and players have control and are required to make quick decisions and solve problems. If you link up to other players online, you can have 'real-life' conversations. There are also physical benefits, such as increased dexterity and coordination – in one study, surgeons who regularly played computer games had a significantly higher accuracy rate than those who didn't. Computer games can also quickly get you into a state of flow, which as we know has countless benefits to our creative lives and general wellbeing (see page 12). The more active games – where you dance out routines or play tennis using a motion-sensitive racquet – can increase fitness almost as well as conventional exercise. You don't need to be a signed-up gamer with a headset, even games on your phones can bring benefits. From word games to problem-solving puzzles and mazes, playing brain games has been shown to improve cognitive function in older players.

Technology is not all bad, and there are many ways you can make it work for you – and have fun with it. (See page 61.)

How to have 100 new ideas

From mixing up your routines and taking more risks to meditating and daydreaming, this chapter has explored lots of ways to encourage quicker, more innovative thinking. But being asked to come up with new ideas can leave many of us frozen, staring at a blank screen or piece of paper in a panic. Suddenly you have no ideas for anything.

To encourage that all-important divergent thinking, first identify the problem you are trying to solve. This may seem more relevant to inventors and scientists, but it applies to creative arts too.

- What do you want to achieve?
- What is it that you are trying to say?
- Who are you speaking to – what do they need to hear?
- How will other people's lives be improved by this?
- Why do they need it NOW?

Really isolate the issue you want to address – be an annoying toddler and keep asking why.

Now work your way through a series of solutions. Use your visual thinking skills (see page 180). Write your ideas in a spider diagram or sketch a series of images – draw 100 boxes and fill each with an idea, building on the previous one.

Now, take a nap (see page 159 for why).

Finally, analyse your ideas. Cross out all the non-starters and highlight the maybes. Try working a few together until you end up with the perfect solution to your niggling problem.

5

MOVE

I'm naturally pretty lethargic. Maybe that's why crafts were so enjoyable for me growing up – I didn't have to leave the house. I had a great part-time job as a gym receptionist as a teen. I got to laze around being friendly to fit people.

Over the years these strange fit people managed to gradually and supportively get me into exercising. It was hell at first. I'd managed to skive PE at school for two whole years. But the trainers made it fun. They'd make up little games and challenges with speed, distance, heart rate zones, imagined zombies chasing me. Holy horror, I began to find it fun! I felt like my mind was moving more quickly. I was firing on all cylinders and ready to see the opportunities for fun around me – and I had the energy to take advantage of them.

The long-term benefits of gentle exercise are obvious – keeping us playing for longer, having fun until we croak. But sometimes it's hard to keep focused on long-term goals. So focus instead on how *immediately* you feel different after doing some movement. Any kind of movement. Stop before you're exhausted and hate it. Just use it to rev you up, to lift your energy and your mood to a more playful one.

I am motivated by trying to understand the *why* behind things. I find the biology of what's going on when we move fascinating. I've delved into straight-up medical research and a more holistic understanding of what movement does for our bodies and mind. Overlaying that with my personal experience of being physical adds up to a deeper understanding of myself, and I learn more every year.

I'm interested in this area because it has been widely varied for me. I've had periods when my energy – and therefore my ability to feel playful and really enjoy life – has been really low. And I've had years where it's been wonderfully high. Why were they so different? What from the outside world affects my inside world so strongly? Or is it vice versa? Does one thing out of kilter throw off the whole show?

I like understanding how all the systems of the body work together: the mechanics of the muscles and bones, the breath and blood.

Ingesting and digestion, bringing nourishment and energy to our cells. Our nervous system and endocrine system. All these complex mechanisms influencing our metabolism, and affecting how we feel.

When I'm lacking playfulness, I work on truly being aware of how I physically feel, and doing things that make me feel better. Eating food that makes my gut feel good, that produces a steady level of good-mood-enhancer serotonin (rather than those sugar highs and crashes). Moving – even just a little bit – wakes me up and makes me want to look after myself more. Light, gentle exercise takes my body into a low-level adrenaline-fuelled sympathetic nervous system which, when I'm finished, moves me into a deeper experience of my parasympathetic – the rest and digest – nervous system. Swinging between these two pleasant modes makes me feel more alive and in balance.

So much of moving is about breathing. We've all heard the advice about going for a brisk walk, just quick enough so you can maintain a conversation. It's about getting your physical body revved up just enough to change how you feel. At times when I find it too overwhelming to get moving, I know I need to get my metabolism going so I can get better-quality relaxation. It's here that I've found consciously connecting to my breathing techniques an absolute game changer. Breathing with awareness will change your body, physically, immediately. We're kicking our metabolism into a steady cruising pace.

Movement can take us out of our heads for a while. When we're concentrating on moving, our overactive minds, with all that endless chatter and noise and overthinking, can have a break. And when our brain isn't overworked with whatever is making us feel anxious, on edge or overwhelmed, we can free ourselves up to be more playful. Movement can also build confidence. We all know how great it feels to take on and conquer a physical task, however small it may seem. And challenging yourself to get out of your comfort zone leads to taking on bigger goals, as we feel more capable and open to new experiences.

Getting moving is about having fun and being playful with your body. It's not about slogging it out down the gym or running up and down hills as fast as you can – unless that's your thing. Enjoy how it feels just to get your body moving.

Movement and the mind

We all know we should be moving more – current UK guidelines recommend adults should take part in some kind of physical activity every day, totalling a minimum of 150 minutes of moderate-intensity movement each week, plus some strength exercises.

That's quite a lot of moving around! We know it's good for our bodies, keeping us healthy and reducing our chances of succumbing to all kinds of illnesses, but it's now also widely known to have enormous benefits for our brains and general wellbeing.

Moving our bodies increases oxygen to the brain, which encourages new brain cells to develop and improves cognitive function. It also releases certain chemicals that can give our mood a welcome lift, while also giving us an energy boost. Regular movement reduces stress, calms anxiety, can help settle an overactive mind and go some way towards easing symptoms of depression. Regularly moving throughout the day has also been shown to help students remember what they learn and adopt a better attitude in school – which is why so much emphasis is placed on running around at breaktime and all those endless PE lessons . . .

Physical movement is also fun! If you've been sitting at your desk all day, there's nothing more pleasing and satisfying for your body than getting up and doing some simple stretches to release the tension or to let off some steam with a quick dance around the office kitchen. It helps break up the tasks of the day (see gamifying on page 124) and is even better if someone else joins you.

A study from Stanford University has also shown that the old advice of 'going for a walk' really can improve creative thinking – by 60 per cent. Their study had people walking inside on a treadmill, while looking at a blank wall, and outside in the fresh air, and both were shown to increase that all-important divergent thinking when asked to perform the unusual uses test (see page 50). It didn't show any benefits for focused thinking, though – where you have to come up with just one solution to a specific problem. Walking is all about getting those creative sparks firing up.

As creative thinking is often linked to our moods, this isn't altogether so surprising. If we're feeling stressed and frustrated at our desks, it's unlikely we'll be in the best frame of mind for producing our most award-winning ideas. Being aware of how we move, how we breathe, how we physically interact with each other and the world around us is vital if we want to feel more playful and creative.

Tiredness isn't an excuse, we're all tired! How movement can energise you

'Yeah, I'm OK. Just a bit tired . . . I've got a lot on at the moment.' How many times have you heard that old excuse for an answer? And how often have you heard yourself say it out loud, apologetically, with a slump of the shoulders and frowny face? Let's call time on the tiredness get-out. Being a playful person is NOT linked to your current energy levels. Playfulness is a state of mind.

So how can we muster up the enthusiasm to resist lying on our sofas watching Netflix and DO something that will make us feel good?

First, remind yourself how positive you feel after you've achieved something – whether that's ticking off a task on your to-do list, spending just half an hour in a creative activity, hanging out with

friends or going for a quick run. Compare that feeling with the complex emotions you cycle through as you wait for the 'next episode' bar to fill during the five-second window of despair, before you're sucked into an hour of someone else's drama. Remember that comparison.

Next, maybe you need to look at why you're feeling so slow. Are you doing all the things you know you should – like drinking enough water, getting your precious eight hours' sleep, eating all those vegetables, exercising, not boozing every night? Or are you downing triple-shot lattes at 11am? You don't need to be told the basics of a healthy lifestyle, so if you're not doing them, start. If you need a reward system to bribe you into new habits, try the life loyalty card on page 127.

Or are you stressed out and anxious? Often life throws us more than we feel we can handle, and that can feel exhausting. Have a think: there could be some simple ways that will provide big changes to ease the pressure. Can you delegate, offload or just say NO?! Or it may be that we can't change much about our circumstances right now – we just have to ride them out and wait for the tide to turn. But how we handle ourselves during those tough times can make a huge difference to our resilience when they inevitably crop up again. Just because we're facing difficulties, doesn't mean we have to think about them 24/7. It's OK to take time out and gain a bit of lightness to our emotions.

Get moving

Moving your body regularly is a well-known antidote to anxiety and an all-round wonder treatment for your health and wellbeing. It significantly reduces our chances of developing all kinds of illnesses, boosts self-esteem and confidence, slows down brain ageing and gives us a big dose of happiness hormones. It can also give us a big injection of energy – even though this seems counter-intuitive until we try it.

You don't have to commit to a high-intensity workout – plenty of studies show how slow movement could be more beneficial to our health (see page 238). A walk around the block, a meandering cycle, some stretching or gentle yoga – anything that gets your body moving will help raise your energy and mood. Even better: do it with friends.

Quick move

Next time you feel your energy levels slip lower than a limbo stick, give one of these a go and feel your tiredness magically disappear, leaving you more time to do all the fun things. Getting physical can also get us into a flow state almost instantly, meeting those key flow requirements of undivided focus and attention.

Step outside

Go for a walk, gentle jog or cycle and gain all the extra benefits of fresh air and sunshine – don't forget your daily dose of vitamin D. Take the unexpected route, look up rather than down at the ground to see things from a fresh perspective. Or create your own GPS picture for added playful points and imaginative thinking power-ups (see page 244).

Let's dance

Make a mood-boosting, energy-lifting, smile-inducing playlist and every time you feel yourself slipping into sluggishness get it on the stereo – or have your own silent disco in the loos at work.

Yoga and meditation

Both these activate a range of different systems in our brains and bodies. Regularly taking a moment to calm and focus our minds, combined with all the physical benefits yoga has to offer, can be just the medicine we need in our modern busy worlds. (See also pages 200 and 240.)

Rock climbing

Want something more challenging? When your mind is focused on NOT falling to your death, it tends to block out other thoughts, keeping you in flow up to the top. Bonus: seeing the world from a different perspective.

Team sports

Five-a-side, netball, hockey, dodgeball, dancing – whatever you fancy. Join a local league for bonus progression points. Working as a team boosts social connections (see page 81).

Jump around

OK, you might want to do this one in private, but for 30 seconds jump around, wave your arms, kick your legs out and stretch your face muscles in a silent exaltation (it sounds weird, but sometimes weird is good) and you'll feel more energetic.

Also check out the other ideas in this chapter:

- Play neighbourhood bingo, page 226.
- Go on your own nature walk, page 225.
- Stretch your downward dog, page 241.
- Make the world your playground with beginner's parkour, page 250.

There's a whole world out there!

While familiarity in your surroundings can be reassuring – knowing your neighbours and the people we interact with can help us feel connected with and part of our community – we also know that routine can be the death of creativity (see page 152). Most of us tend to tread the same paths throughout the week, and our interests and to-do lists dictate the places we go, what we see and the people we talk to along the way.

We may notice that we are now shuffling through some fallen leaves in autumn, are squinting at a particularly perfect blue sky in summer, or, on a really exceptional day, we may catch a glimpse of some blossoms in a refection of a window in the evening sun, but sometimes we need a bit more of a nudge to realise that our local environment has lots to offer us visually.

Look up at the buildings and spot a piece of history you never noticed before – maybe there's some old ghost signage painted on the wall or some decorative architecture above your local pound shop. Let it encourage you to think about your place in history and gain perspective on your situation. Take a side road and discover a new park or whole part of town you didn't know was there before. Walk over bridges to see the world from new heights. There's nature thriving wherever you are too – in front gardens, between the paving stones, on abandoned plots, along the edges of the railway – it has an amazing tenacity and grows even in adversity – a lesson we could probably all do with learning.

'Play is the highest form of research.'
Albert Einstein

Depending on where you live, some of what you see may be more sensually pleasing than elsewhere, but if you look hard enough there are signs of all kinds of life to be appreciated all around us. Approach the world around you as though you're seeing it for the first time, every time.

Open the front door and play neighbourhood bingo – you can play this solo or with a group – taking photos and sharing them as you tick off the card.

BINGO

TELEPHONE
TELEPHONE
An old red phone box
Fixed wheel bike
Yellow car
Person in unseasonal clothing
Plant pot on a doorstep
Blue front door
Squirrel
Jogger
Maimed pigeon
Bin-dipping seagull
Bird song (listen hard)
Scaffolding

A tree trunk so big you can't wrap your arms around it
A purple flower
A pair of dogs
An out-of-service bus
A busker
A symmetrical house
A lost shopping trolley
Fast-food wrappers
Paper coffee cup
Gum on the floor
Road works
Poop (any variety)
A cactus in a window
Hanging plant pot
THE PORCUPINE
A pub with an animal in the name

Up-cycled washable tote bag

When you're out and about, have a rummage in a charity shop for a XL t-shirt. Even if secondhand clothes are not your usual style you don't need to be too precious about finding a shirt that you like for this. Weird printed ones are fun, or a colour might just call to you. It's particularly fun if you are in another country, where the printed t-shirts they have might are a little different to ones you usually see and you get a useful different memento from your trip. It's a great little project to do with a little gang of you!

Materials needed

- 1 adult-size t-shirt (medium size minimum – or else the bag is too small! I use size large or x-large)
- 1 pair of full-size scissors
- A pair of working hands on a human body

1. Cut out the neck seam a couple of centimetres from the seam itself to create a collarless neckline. This is the bag opening.
2. Trim off the very bottom seam so it has a clean, straight edge with no thick seam.
3. Cut the arms off, from the body side of the seam so that you get rid of the seam. Discard the arms. Your t-shirt should now look like a 'muscle tank top'.

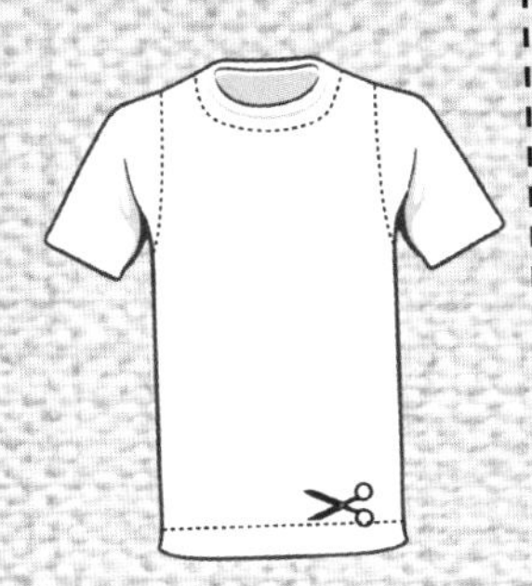

4. Cut 2cm-wide strips up from the bottom waist of the shirt towards the top. Cut both the back and front of the shirt together so the strips line up. Make the cuts 10–15 cm long. This will create a dangly thread/fabric strip look, also known as fringe. The longer the strips, the less space you'll have in your bag – you've been warned!
5. Pull on the strips so they become slightly longer and skinnier. They should naturally curl up a little, and become noodle-like.

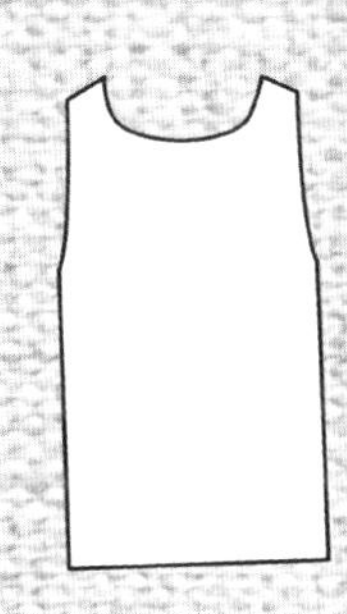

6. Match up the first front strip with the first back strip. You are going to tie this in a double knot. Do the same with the second front and second back strips, etc. Continue going down the line of strips. This will close off and secure the bottom of your bag.
7. Cut the top seam of the shoulder straps in half. This way, you have four straps to work with: a left front and back and a right front and back.

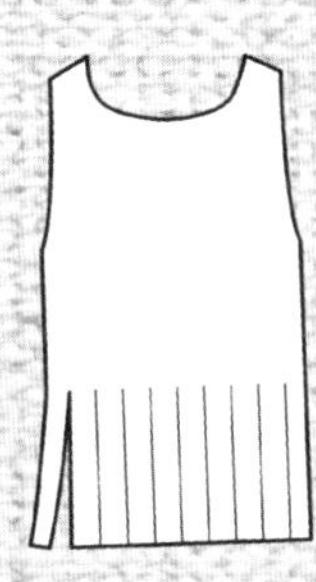

8. Tie the front left and the front right in a knot. Then, tie the back left and the back right in a knot, too. This creates the two handles for your bag.

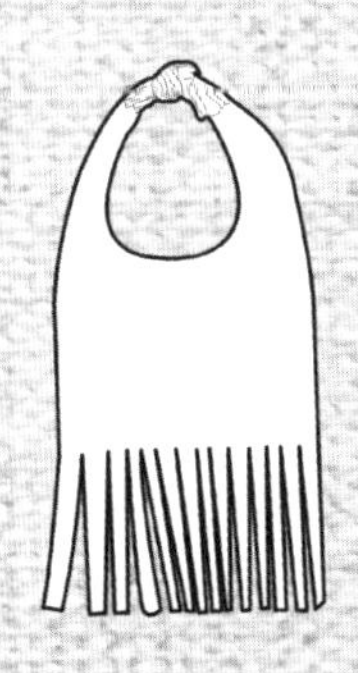

Note: if you're not a fan of the fringe, you can turn the t-shirt inside out before you get started. Cut the strips only 5–10 cm deep, tie the fringe knots and cut off the excess, leaving just a couple of centimetres. Turn your t-shirt back inside out, and you can't see the fringe!

If you're using a regular cotton t-shirt, the bag is washable! Perfect for your gym kit.

EXPERT IN PLAY

PAUL WOOD
THESTREETTREE.COM

Paul Wood is the author of London's Street Trees, and London is a Forest. He writes the blog thestreettree.com – you can follow him @thestreettree.

Even if you live in the middle of a busy town or city, you may be surprised by how much nature can be found on your doorstep.

I've lived in London for over twenty-five years, but I grew up surrounded by trees in bosky Kent. I spent my childhood playing in the woods: climbing trees, building dens and playing hide-and-seek among the copses, thickets and spinneys. Playing in nature comes very naturally to children, even if they just have a back garden or a local park, and as I grew up, I became increasingly fascinated by the natural communities of trees, plants and animals that surrounded me. I would spend as much time as I could playing – and learning – outdoors in the woods, a wondrous playground-cum-classroom with no teachers or homework to spoil the fun.

Eventually, I swapped the woods for the concrete jungle, and soon I was beginning to notice a whole new environment: the urban forest – all the trees and green spaces in a town or city. In London, a staggering 47 per cent of the city's area is green or blue, and remarkably, urban areas host a huge diversity of plant species, the most noticeable of which are, of course, the trees. Hundreds of different species thrive in parks, gardens and even won the streets of our urban areas. Once I started noticing them, I got hooked on surveying my surroundings from a whole new arboreal perspective.

It started at work. I would spend my lunchtimes exploring the streets near my office, and soon I had discovered all manner of rare and exotic trees within a few minutes' walk. Trees have been planted in cities for centuries, and in London, the Victorians set about the task with gusto. By 1870, swathes of the city were being systematically planted with trees, most notably, London planes (actually they were popularised in Paris, but because of the sheer numbers planted in London at this time, they picked up their 'London' bit). Since then, urban tree planters have really gone to town, and now over 400 species and cultivars can be found on the streets of London alone.

I discovered strawberry trees, mimosa and a Persian silk tree near London Bridge. When I moved offices to Oxford Street, there was a whole new urban ecosystem to explore: fascinating 250-year-old London plane trees in Mayfair and Bhutan pines in Soho. During a stint in Brighton, I became familiar with the city's remarkable elm population. There are thousands of big, old trees on the streets that miraculously survived the ravages of Dutch Elm Disease in the 1970s. And in rather less genteel Deptford, I saw how nature can not only take advantage of, but thrive in any derelict post-industrial plot of land it gets half a chance to colonise.

For me, the city is just as fascinating and, in some places, as beautiful, as the countryside. I walk round the city to see what's growing whenever I can, I regularly get off the bus or Tube a stop or two early, and I once led the company I worked for on a two-mile nature walk through Regent's Park to an office party in Camden Town.

You don't need me to tell you there are great physical and mental health benefits to being outdoors, so if football in the park isn't your thing, maybe looking more closely at the nature that surrounds us could be. Studies have shown that being close to nature – be that your local park, your back garden, or perhaps even the trees on your street

– can be such a positive step for all of us. Being in nature can improve our mood, it gives us joy and can help us put things in perspective. So, even in the depths of winter there's nothing like a hike round the park looking out for birds, not to mention the strange beauty of all those leafless trees.

To get you started, here's a few things to look out for:

Winter: migrating birds and early flowers

You might spot species like goldcrests in the bushes and, if you're very lucky, beautiful waxwings gorging on the berries of a street tree. Fragrant mimosa trees will flower in January or February, while snowdrops and crocuses can be seen in woods and grassy areas.

Spring: trees really start coming into their own

Magnolias start blooming in March, and by the end of the month, cherry trees will be beginning to flower too. Not to be outdone, less showy deciduous trees put out their leaves in abundant, fresh greens. For me, beech trees are one of the loveliest.

Summer: the season of plenty

A time to appreciate the billowing beauty of big trees in the verdant landscape. Walking along the banks of slow-moving rivers can be particularly relaxing at this time of year; you might see willows and poplars, while dragonflies dart over the water.

Autumn: spectacular colour

Towns and cities are particularly good places to see some of the most dazzling trees during October and November. Common street tree species like crimson American sweetgum, claret Raywood ash or golden Norway maple are worth looking out for.

Leaf cutting

These are super pretty to add to a card, or to hang somewhere where they can dangle with the light behind them.

You will need:

- A few nice leaves
- A superfine felt-tip pen
- A scalpel with a fresh blade
- A cutting board (or a kitchen chopping board will do)

1

Make sure your leaves are clean and dry before you start.

2

Use a fine felt-tip pen to trace a design on to one of your leaves. Go for a design with only small elements to cut out at first, so you can practise your cutting skills.

3

Make sure you keep all the big veins on the leaf intact, to keep it together. Shade the areas to cut out.

4

Start with the smallest elements of the design first. This is because the leaf will have more strength when there isn't much cut out. Using your scalpel and cutting mat, cut out the design, working away from your fingers. Use the point of the knife to remove the pieces as you go. Finish by cutting out and removing any larger pieces, still keeping the big veins intact.

Pressing flowers

1

Pick some flowers on your walk. Preferably flat ones! Choose flowers that are either still in bud form, or that are freshly bloomed.

2

Hydrate your flowers. Cut the stems at an angle, remove the lower leaves, put in a vase with teaspoon of sugar for a few hours. Remove and dry the stems. If you have something bigger, like a rose, you might need to cut it in half with a scalpel.

3

Arrange your flowers between a few layers of face tissue or another absorbent paper so they are not touching. Kitchen towel has patterns that might show on the petals of some flowers.

4

Find a heavy old book with no staples or any other metal. Sandwich your flowers in it. Zap it in the microwave for 30 seconds. Let it cool for a minute, change the paper and zap it again.

5

Change the paper. Find the heaviest things you can to weigh them down. Maybe bricks, more books, a tower of tinned tomatoes or the workout weight you left under your bed this past year.

6

Change the paper every few days for two to three weeks until the flowers are completely dry.

7

Or, to speed it up, iron them! Make sure there is no water in the iron. The last thing you want to do is add moisture to the flower. Heat the iron on low. Once warm, press the iron on top of the upper sheet of paper for 10 to 15 seconds. You do not need to move it about. Wait for another 15 seconds until the paper has cooled, then repeat this process.

8

Carefully lift the paper to check if the flower is stiff and dry. When removing, use a pair of tweezers, or very carefully use your fingers, as a completely dry flower is very delicate.

9

Glue to card and frame or send to a friend.

Slow movement, fast thinking

Imagine a raging dinosaur chasing you through a forest while you're being shouted at from the sidelines by that teacher from school who used to give you nightmares. This isn't all that far from what your body feels like when you do those #SMASHINGIT high-intensity workouts and bootcamp sessions you love so much.

While HIIT workouts have been linked to speedier weight loss as well as some other health benefits, like more balanced blood sugar levels, they also activate our flight-or-flight response, raising cortisol and adrenaline in the process. Coming from a stressful day at work, where we're overloaded with information from all sides, and then battering your body with yet more stress in the form of a metaphorical hungry T-Rex means we're on constant high alert without ever really switching off. Over time, this endless chasing of hits and HIIT can cause havoc with our hormones, sleep and digestion.

We maybe need to have a bit of a rethink about why we exercise. Although it can feel like we're de-stressing by pounding it out at a spin class to nineties' tunes, we should actually be looking for ways to balance out the stress that daily life already gives us. We need to s…l…o…w… down and calm our nervous systems, not add more fuel to the flames.

Our focus should be on regulating our breathing, realigning our bent-over posture, improving our flexibility to counteract all the hours we spend in one position and calming the F down. Going from 0–100 is also more likely to cause us injuries – instead, we need to be more in tune with what our body really needs. Taking the time to focus on what we are really feeling means our body and mind become more in sync. And when our bodies are in balance, they're also less likely to hang on to fat in case of troubled times ahead. So if weight loss is your goal then you could be going about it all wrong. As an added bonus, allowing time for our minds to settle and wander may also be just what we need to solve a problem or come up with creative new ideas. It's unlikely anyone comes up with ingenious solutions to creative problems when they're under attack from a man-eating reptile.

If you really love your CrossFit, don't deny yourself your dopamine high, but just make sure to balance it out with a bit of much-needed restorative calm. It's slow movement that is key here, at a pace where you can talk or sing comfortably. Walking, Pilates, yoga – but not the really intense kind – are all the kinds of restorative exercises we should be aiming for. Yin yoga especially, where you hold poses for several minutes, really allows you to check in with what's going on with your body and helps regulate your breathing. On the following pages is a perfect yoga sequence to calm down that overactive mind and body.

Also check out the breathing exercise and meditation on pages 132 and 200.

Yoga flow

Breathe deeply into your belly for five breaths. Sitting cross-legged, interlace your fingers and push your palms to the sky. Keeping your back upright, bend to the right and take five breaths. Slowly come up, then bend to the left and take five breaths.

Cross your legs the other way for the **seated twist.** Turn your chest to the right and let your right hand go to the earth behind you and your left hand to your right knee. Breathe into your belly and as you exhale, squeeze your belly in and try to use the belly muscles to exaggerate the twist. Now exhale, using the strength of your arms to twist deeper. Take three more breaths, feeling the twist move through your spine. Gently come back to centre and repeat on the left.

Get on your hands and knees for **cat and cow.** Inhale, drop your belly and look up. Exhale, look at your navel and tuck in your tailbone. Move between these positions for five breaths, focusing on your upper back. Draw your shoulder blades together and down as you look up, and push the floor away as you look down.

Step your right foot to the outside of your right hand. Keep the inside of your knee touching the outside of your arm. Let your elbows soften as you sink into your hips for **lizard pose.** Feel the stretch in your right hip. Keep your spine long, gaze forward. Imagine your breastbone moving to the floor. Take five breaths.

Keeping your legs where they are, bring your torso upright, hook your thumbs together and lift your hands over your head with straight arms. Sink into your front knee, squeeze your bum and hold this **crescent moon lunge;** feel the stretch across the front of your left hip for five breaths.

Take your hands to the floor and your right leg back to match the left. Repeat on the left side.

Take five breaths in **child's pose**: bring your bum to your heels and forehead to the floor with arms stretched out in front.

Tuck your toes under, and keeping your lower back in a straight line, lift your pelvis up by straightening the legs: you're now in **downward-facing dog**. Stay there for five breaths.

Step gently at the top of your mat and with knees bent let your spine dangle down from your hips. Sway from side to side. Walk your hands up your legs until you are standing. Stand taller, pushing your big toes down and pulling your shoulders back and down until you are standing strong like a **mountain.** Lengthen the back of your neck until you get a double chin. Big toes touching, squeeze the knees together. Lift your arms over your head and sit down in an imaginary chair behind you. Draw your belly in and lengthen the small of your back. Sit lower and squeeze your bum into **chair pose.** Take deep breaths, feel the burn. Return to standing.

For **warrior two,** step your left leg behind you, let the heel drop so your foot points out to the side. With hips open to the side, bend deep into your right leg. Stretch your arms out at shoulder height. Make it feel fiery in your legs. Take strong breaths, face relaxed. Repeat on the other side.

Now for the most famous yoga pose: **tree pose**. Lift your right knee up to your hip and open your knee to the side. Place your foot to the inside of your left leg above or below the knee. Don't rest your foot in the nook of your left knee – use your right bum. Focus your gaze on a point in front of you. Feel the left foot correct the wobble without consciously doing it with your mind. Let the breath return to the belly. Take ten big breaths, then switch to the other side.

Take a big step out so you have legs wide apart, toes slightly closer than heels. With hands on hips, lift the heart, bend your knees and fold forward, walking your hands down your legs in **wide-legged forward bend**. Try to keep your spine long, hinging at the hips. Take big deep breaths – aim to stretch your ribcage!

Return to upright, then bring your hands down to the top of the mat and position your feet to the back into **plank**. Draw your belly in and push the mat away. Push through your heels, soften your face and hold until your breath gets really hard. Lower yourself onto your front with control.

Lie on your front, hands either side of your hips, palms down. Point your toes, squeeze your bum and lift your spine away from the floor, neck long. Try to get your little fingers to touch above your bum. This is **locust pose.** Inhales make you longer, exhales lift you higher. Take five breaths, then lower down and roll onto your back.

Lie on your back, knees bent, feet grounded. Press your hands down either side of your hips. Push your feet down, tuck your tailbone under and slowly lift your pelvis, lower back, then upper back away from the earth into **bridge**. Interlace your fingers behind your back and push down to lift higher. Squeeze your knees, breathe, then slowly lower: upper back, lower back, then pelvis. Extend your legs. Let your feet flop out to the sides. Bring your

hands slightly away from your hips, palms face up. Adjust until comfortable. This is **corpse pose**, so no moving. Slacken your jaw, let your eyeballs sink into your head. Notice how it feels to be still. Take 20 uncontrolled breaths. Notice your body, thoughts and feelings without judgement.

When you're ready, do a big 'morning' stretch from fingertips to toes. Hug your knees into your chest and roll to one side. Gently push yourself up to seated. Bring your palms together in gratitude for your body and for yourself for doing something kind for you.

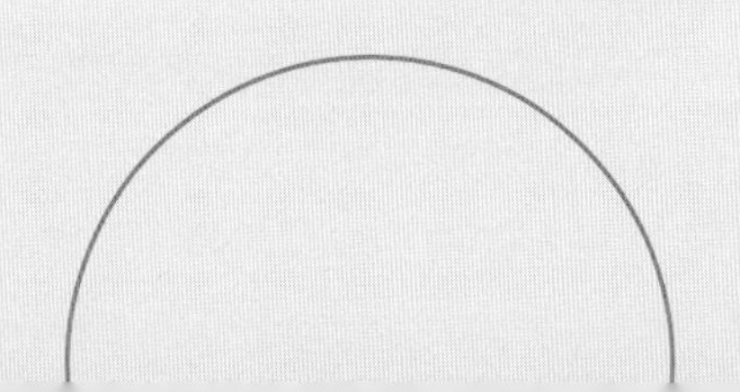

Mapping shapes on a run using GPS

Make exercising another opportunity to be creative and playful, and stretch your spacial awareness at the same time. Reimagine your daily run, dog walk, cycle or stroll in the park and paint a picture while you do it. Set up a fitness tracker, look at your map ahead of time and sketch out your chosen image – a dog, a smiley face, a message to a loved one, a penis – however you want to express your creativity, it's totally up to you – then draw over the route with your feet. There are some great inspirations to find online – and if you are a keen cyclist you can cover even more ground.

Challenge accepted!

Testing your physical capabilities and pushing yourself perhaps beyond what you consider to be your personal limitations is an instantly gratifying way to prove you are more than you think you are. Especially as we get older, we can often find ourselves becoming a bit stuck in our routines – the same gym class, jogging distance, dog-walking circuit of the park.

Realising we are physically more capable than we thought we were is a huge and instant confidence boost. Most of the perceived limitations we place on ourselves are totally made up in our heads – either based on what other people have told us we can or cannot do, or what that chatty, unhelpful voice in our head has somehow made us believe. Excuses for not giving something a go while we sit frustrated at home range from worrying that we'll fail at it, feeling overwhelmed by the enormity of starting, having a desire for perfection where anything less is a catastrophe, and fearing other people's thoughts and criticisms on our less-than-noteworthy performance.

It's time to stop caring what other people think and to stop aiming for perfect. Most people are far more concerned with what they're doing themselves anyway to really notice what you're up to. And anyone who would bother to criticise or judge someone else for giving something a go is obviously dealing with a load of their own self-esteem issues and we should perhaps think about offering them a helping hand.

Regret for not doing something is always so much worse than feeling like you never tried. And other people seeing you achieve new goals will make you an inspiration for them too!

Marathon runners often report huge benefits across their whole lives – from better time management due to all those painful training plans, an increased ability to overcome obstacles and challenges that arise, and knowing how to break larger goals into smaller ones by celebrating those milestones along the way (a bit like gamifying on page 124). And, of course, there's that overwhelming feeling of achievement – a high that they then go on to chase at work and in other personal goals.

Running a marathon may not be your thing at all, and even if it is, it of course feels like a huge undertaking when you first start to think about it. And that's because it is. But training for a 26.2-mile run is the perfect example of how everything starts with a few laps of the park, metaphorical or otherwise. And that's the whole point. You just have to make a start, however small that is. Then each time you find yourself getting comfy, push yourself a little bit more.

Feeling slightly scared about something and then realising you can overcome it will make you feel more at ease with testing yourself in other areas of your life. Soon your baseline of normality will be raised and you'll be conquering the world!

Test yourself physically as well as mentally and stretch to your actual potential – not the potential you think you have or that someone else might have once told you you have.

Do it with someone else

Although this is about your personal goals, it can be more fun to do it together, plus you're less likely to bail.

Do it in private

No one needs to know – this is not for show-and-tell.

Wear some fun outfits

Who says you can't be Wonder Woman in your street dance class?

Be more kid

Kids don't care about looking stupid. There's no such thing. They just learn from each other and give the monkey bars another go tomorrow.

Remember how great it felt to overcome a challenge in the past?

You can do it again! Choose a small goal and then go for it.

Get happy with setbacks

We all know by now that learning through challenges is the best way to grow. They're not failed attempts, they're just steps along the way to hone your skills (see also page 176). Plus everyone loves a funny story about when things went wrong . . .

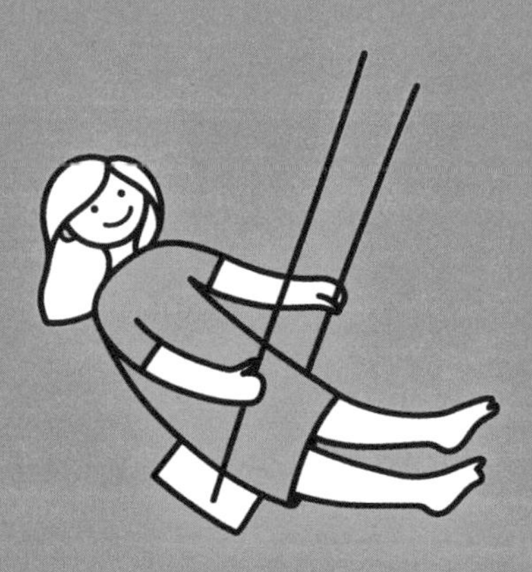

EXPERT IN PLAY

DAN EDWARDES
PARKOUR GENERATIONS

Parkour: Movement Mastery

I grew up running, jumping and climbing through the forests of West Sussex, in England, so it was only natural for me to embrace the movement philosophy of parkour when I discovered it as an adult in 2001.

Parkour quickly opened my eyes to how I could apply the principles of natural human movement to any environment – even an urban one. Cities soon became my playground, and I found my body and mind challenged and stretched like never before – balance, agility, functional strength, explosive power, mobility; every aspect of your physicality improves when you train in parkour, as it draws on the immense, innate potential for athleticism that resides in all of us.

I have taught parkour all over the world over the past 15 years, and the benefits it brings to people from all walks of life and of all ages and abilities are very clear to me. These include not only increased holistic health and fitness, but a deeper connection with one's own body through improved coordination, spatial awareness and adaptation. Even more importantly, it brings about a powerful psychological shift, owing to increased confidence, courage and willpower, and an enhanced perception of space, places and the world around us.

I truly believe parkour is a practice that captures and expands on the vast potential of the human body, and it reveals to us just how limitless our movement potential can be.

Parkour Training Practices

Rail walking

To develop your mobile balance and stability, practise walking along low railings of varying width until you are comfortable with even, thin, round railings. Start on railings close to the ground. Keep your feet in line with the rail, arms out to the side at shoulder height, and maintain proper control during every step. Be precise with your movements and use your arms to minimise sway in the body. For extra difficulty, try to turn 180 degrees without coming off the railing.

Step vault

Approach a waist-high wall or other obstacle. Place one hand on the obstacle while you bring the opposite leg to step up onto it. Be sure with your hand and foot placement, and try to be light on the obstacle as you pass over it. Don't rush! Lift your trailing leg up and pass it beneath your body and over the obstacle to step down on the other side. Repeat, using the other arm and leg.

Precision jump

Find two points on the ground that you can jump between safely that are within your maximum jump range (a raised pavement edge is a great landing spot). Push from both feet and jump to that spot, landing on the balls of your feet and absorbing the impact by flexing the knees and sitting back into the landing, similar to a standard squat pattern, with your feet stacked under your hips or narrower. Jump back to finish the drill, then repeat in sets of five.

Sources

INTRODUCTION

'Games Animals Play', Carl Zimmer, *Forbes*, 14 Dec 2006.
'Flow and the Foundations of Positive Psychology', Mihaly Csikszentmihalyi, Springer Science+Business Media Dordrecht, 2014.

1: CREATE

Do You Doodle?
'What does doodling do?', Jackie Andrade, *Applied Cognitive Psychology*, Feb 2009.
'The Miseducation of the Doodle', Sunni Brown, *A List Apart*, Jan 2011.
'Doodles may reveal our subconscious thoughts, says graphologist', Rob Knight, *Independent*, 10 Aug 2018.

Hands On
'How busy hands can alter our brain chemistry', *CBS News*, 18 Mar 2018.
'Do or DIY', Kelly Lambert, *RSA Journal*, Issue 1, 2015.
'Creativity, Happiness and Your Own Two Hands', Carrie Barron, *Psychology Today*, May 2012.
'Do or DIY', Kelly Lambert, *RSA Journal*, Issue 1, 2015.
http://www.faybutler.com/wwfdhand.htm

Be More Wonderfully Weirdo
'Novelty seeking is linked to openness and extraversion, and can lead to greater creative performance', Małgorzata A. Gocłowska et al, *Journal of Personality*, Mar 2018.
'Diversifying experiences enhance cognitive flexibility', Simone M. Ritter, Rodica Ioana Damian, Dean Keith Simonton, Rick Van Baaren et al, *Journal of Experimental Social Psychology*, Jul 2012, 48(4), 961–964.
'Connections From Kafka: Exposure to Meaning Threats Improves Implicit Learning of an Artificial Grammar', Travis Proulx, Steven J. Heine, *Psychological Science*, Sep 2009.
'How Enlightened Leaders Are Borrowing From Improv Comedy To Boost Team Creativity', Forbes, 26 Nov 2020
www.sparringmind.com/creative-thinking

Think surreal
'The Structure of Intellect, J.P. Guilford, *Psychological Bulletin*, 1956. 53(4): p. 267–293/

Laugh Your Way to Creative Genius
'How Enlightened Leaders Are Borrowing From Improv Comedy To Boost Team Creativity', Forbes, 26 Nov 2020
'Haha and aha!: creativity, idea generation, improvisational humor,

and product design', Barry Matthew Kudrowitz, *Massachussetts Institute of Technology*, 2010.

Technology is the Death of All Creativity
'Is technology making us more creative?', Tomas Chamorro-Premuzic, *The Guardian*, 18 Jun 2015.
'Information and imagination: why technology isn't killing creativity', James Ingram, *Raconteur*, 10 Aug 2018.
'Cities: how crowded life is changing us', Gaia Vince, *BBC Future*, 17 May 2003.
'Want to boost creativity? Try playing Minecraft', Iowa State University, *Science Daily*, 8 Jul 2019.
'Instagram by the Numbers: Stats, Demographics & Fun Facts', *Omnicore*, 20 Oct 2020.

2: CONNECT

Connect with New People
'This Study of 300,000 People Reveals the 1 Secret to Living a Longer, Healthier Life', Jeff Haden, *Inc.*, 17 Oct 2017.
'Dunbar's number: Why we can only maintain 150 relationships', Christine Ro, *BBC Future*, 9 Oct 2019.
'Group flow: How can teams experience "flow" together?', www.bakadesuyo.com

Organised fun
https://www.gamingzion.com/gambling/gambling-news/brief-history-dice/
https://www.interaction-design.org/literature/article/a-brief-history-of-games

Play with your food
'We eat 60 per cent of our meals in front of the TV and a third admit not making any conversation', *Mail Online*, 13 Mar 2013.
'You Won't Believe the Super Relatable Way the Queen Eats Dinner', Christina Montford, *Showbiz CheatSheet*, 5 Oct 2019.
'Is the dining room in decline', Olivia Heath, *House Beautiful*, 20 Sep 2017.
'A Sad Tale of Family Meal Times', Tefal, 25 Jan 2018.
'How Cooking at Home Can Make You More Productive at Work', Derek Loosvelt, *Vault*, 16 May 2018.

3: IMAGINE

Imagining your future – dream big!
'To Reach Your Goal, Make a Mental Movie', Srini Pillay, *Harvard Business Review*, 5 Mar 2014.

Gamifying
'The Play Theory of Hunter-Gatherer Egalitarianism', Peter Gray, *Psychology Today*, Aug 2019.

Reading is the easiest way to activate our imaginations
'Reading books is on the decline', Michael Kozlowski, *GoodEReader*, 14 Jul 2018.
'Why We Don't Read, Revisited', Caleb Crain, *The New Yorker*, 14 Jun 2018, https://www.newyorker.com/culture/cultural-comment/why-we-dont-read-revisited
'Why our future depends on libraries, reading and daydreaming', Neil Gaiman, *The Guardian*, 15 Oct 2013.
'Telling the China Story: The Rise and Rise of Chinese Science Fiction', Gautham Shenoy, *Factor Daily*, 12 Jan 2019.

4: THINK

Learning through play
The United Nations Convention on the Rights of the Child, 2 Sep 1990.
'Play is more than just fun', Stuart Brown, Ted Talks 2008.
'Humans produce new brain cells throughout their lives, say researchers', Nicola Davis, *The Guardian*, 5 Apr 2018.

Make time for daydreaming
'A Wandering Mind Is an Unhappy Mind', Matthew A. Killingsworth and Daniel T. Gilbert, *Science*, 12 Nov 2010.
'Ode to positive constructive daydreaming', Rebecca L McMillan, Scott Barry Kaufman, Jerome L. Singer, *Frontiers in Psychology*, 23 Sep 2013.
'Five Surprising Facts About Daydreaming', Christine Dell'Amore, *National Geographic*, 16 Jul 2013.
'Here's How To Daydream Your Way To Success', Drake Baer, *Business Insider*, 2 May 2014.

A playful mind: think fun – how to change your mood when you're not in the mood
'People were happier in 1957 than today, according to research', *Mental Health Today*, 23 Jan 2017.
'Optimism and Its Impact on Mental and Physical Well-Being', Ciro Conversano, Alessandro Rotondo et al, *Clinical Practice & Epidemiology in Mental Health*, 14 May 2010.
'Why being an optimist is good for your heart', *CTV News*, 28 Sep 2019.
'How Enlightened Leaders Are Borrowing From Improv Comedy To Boost Team Creativity', Forbes, 26 Nov 2020
'The Power of Humor in Ideation and Creativity', Moses Ma, *Psychology Today*, 17 Jun 2004.

Risky business
'Sir James Dyson: From barrows to billions', BBC News, 22 Jan 2019

Surprise!
'Want to Innovate? Science Says, Be Spontaneous', Dr KH Kim, Creativity Post, 21 Feb 2017.
'This is Your Brain on Jazz: Researchers Use MRI to Study Spontaneity, Creativity', *John Hopkins Medicine*, 26 Feb 2008.

Meditation and creative thinking
'14 Amazing Benefits of Meditation That Can Actually Rewire Your Brain', *Science of People*.
'The Buddhist and the Neuroscientist', Kathy Gilsinan, *The Atlantic*, 4 Jul 2015.
'Brains of Buddhist monks scanned in meditation study', Matt Danzico, *BBC News*, 24 Apr 2011.
'How Mindful Meditation Boosts Creative Innovation', Bianca Rothschild, *Huffpost*, 25 Jul 2014.
'Prior Meditation Practice Modulates Performance and Strategy Use in Convergent- and Divergent-Thinking Problems', Lorenza S. Colzato, Ayca Szapora, Dominique Lippelt, Bernhard Published online: 29 October 2014 # Springer Science+Business Media New York 2014.

Dreams
'What Can We Learn From Our Dreams?', Martine Thompson, *Vogue*, 16 Jan 2018.

Technology and what it's doing to our brains
'8 Ways Tech Has Completely Rewired Our Brains', Rebecca Hiscott, *Mashable UK*, 14 Mar 2014.
'Surgeons With Video Game Skill Appear To Perform Better In Simulated Surgery

Skills Course', Jama and Archives Journals, *ScienceDaily*, 20 Feb 2007.

5: MOVE

Movement and the mind
'Stanford study finds walking improves creativity', May Wong, *Stanford News*, 24 Apr 2014.

Tiredness isn't an excuse, we're all tired!

How movement can energise you
'Effects of Exercise and Physical Activity on Anxiety', Elizabeth Anderson and Geetha Shivakumar, *Frontiers in Psychiatry*, 23 Apr 2013.
'The effect of acute resistance exercise on feelings of energy and fatigue', Matthew Herring, Patrick O'Connor, *Journal of Sports Sciences*, 20 May 2009.

THANK YOUS

Firstly, thank you to my writer Laura Bayliss – it was so much fun working with you at the Standard.

To all the contributors: Jen Hacking, Ruth and Jesse Dupre, Kate Phillipson, Poppy Schooling, Brandy Kingelpuss, Soumya Thomas, Melody Travers, Samantha Medlycott, Kim Leadbeater MBE, Jonathan Cranston, Tristan Williams, Dr Gareth Moore, Paul Wood, Dan Edwardes.

The wonderful Lydia, Sarah and Harriet at HarperCollins and Sim in the incredibly patient design team.

Thank you to my Art Club co-founder Siri Betts and our crew Stephanne, Adele, Britta, Matt Bucknal, Henry and Joe. All my creative teachers.

My mum and dad, Sarah and Jonathan, Sophia. Jessica Boughton and Valine Barhar. Stew and Shan and Jono and all the yogis. Including my awesome agent Rachel Mills and Helen Russell-Clark who introduced me to her.

My Drink, Shop, Do co-founder Kristie Bishop; Bianca Hepworth and the original gangsters, Linsey Cockburn and dream team, Amy Laker and the build-it-back-better beauties.

Oh and Max Halley. Who plays hardest of all.

HarperCollins*Publishers*
1 London Bridge Street
London SE1 9GF

www.harpercollins.co.uk

HarperCollins*Publishers*
1st Floor, Watermarque Building,
Ringsend Road, Dublin 4, Ireland

First published by
HarperCollins*Publishers* 2021

10 9 8 7 6 5 4 3 2 1

A catalogue record of this book is available from the British Library

ISBN 978-0-00-839290-1

Printed and bound in Latvia

MIX
Paper from responsible sources
FSC™ C007454

This book is produced from independently certified FSC™ paper to ensure responsible forest management.

For more information visit: www.harpercollins.co.uk/green

Picture credits

All images supplied by Shutterstock.com and Coralie Sleap, with the exception of:

pages 46, 58: CSA Images/Getty Images; 66: Tara Moore/Getty Images; pages 78, 80–81: CSA Images/Getty Images; pages 102–103: © Molu Designs; page 106: CSA Images/Getty Images; page 133: © Melody Travers; pages 146–147: © The Robin Collective; page 154: alashi/Getty Images; page 156: CSA Images/Getty Images; page 159: CSA-Printstock/Getty Images; pages 160–161: © Samantha Medlycott; pages 166–167: bulentgultek/Getty Images; pages 186–189: © Big Potato Games; pages 210, 224: CSA Images/Getty Images.